Early Church History

Zondervan Quick-Reference Library

ZONDERVAN
QUICK
REFERENCE
LIBRARY

Early Church History

Verlyn D. Verbrugge

ZondervanPublishingHouse
Grand Rapids, Michigan

A Division of HarperCollins*Publishers*

Requests for information should be addressed to:

🏛 ZondervanPublishingHouse
Grand Rapids, Michigan 49530

Library of Congress Cataloging-in-Publication Data

Verbrugge, Verlyn D.
    Early church history / Verlyn D. Verbrugge.
        p. cm. — (Zondervan quick-reference library)
    ISBN: 0-310-20395-3 (softcover)
    1. Church history—Primitive and early church, ca. 80-600. I. Title. II. Series.
BR145.2.V47 1998
270.1-dc 21   97-45992
                                                  CIP

Interior design by Sue Vandenberg Koppenol

Printed in the United States of America

---

98 99 00 01 02 03 04 /❖ DC/ 10 9 8 7 6 5 4 3 2 1

Contents

Preface

If someone were to write a history of the church in the twentieth century, he or she would undoubtedly write about great personalities (such as Billy Graham), great theologians (such as Karl Barth), significant churches (such as the Crystal Cathedral), important controversies (such as the liberal-fundamentalist controversy), and concern over church unity (the ecumenical movement). The story of the church in the first century is no different. It is the story of great personalities (such as Peter), great theologians (such as Paul), significant churches (such as the church in Ephesus), important controversies (such as the conflict between the Judaizers and Paul over the salvation of the Gentiles), and concern over church unity (such as Paul's instructions to the Corinthians).

For the most part, with little else to guide us except the New Testament, it is difficult to write a comprehensive history of the church in the first century (see the unit on "Sources"). This book is an attempt to incorporate Acts to Revelation into a continuous story. In such a task, there are many scholarly problems, especially regarding the dating and provenance of New Testament letters. The intent of this book is not to discuss these issues. I have made scholarly decisions on them, which I will assume but not argue for (for example, does Galatians 2:1–10 refer to the Council of Jerusalem in Acts 15 or to Paul's earlier famine visit of Acts 11?). Another person writing a similar book would undoubtedly construct things differently from what I have done. But in the main, the general flow as recorded here of what happened to the church during the first century is accurate.

I would like to thank John Sailhamer for allowing me to write this book in the *Zondervan Quick-Reference Library*. (He did the other seven, and I served as the editor of them.) I am grateful also to the Zondervan editorial department for their confidence in my qualifications to write this book, and especially to Jim Ruark, who did a marvelous job with his editorial pen. I trust this series will be a blessing to many who want to have a bird's-eye view of various disciplines of theology and biblical studies.

Abbreviations of the Books of the Bible

Genesis	Gen.	Nahum	Nah.
Exodus	Ex.	Habakkuk	Hab.
Leviticus	Lev.	Zephaniah	Zeph.
Numbers	Num.	Haggai	Hag.
Deuteronomy	Deut.	Zechariah	Zech.
Joshua	Josh.	Malachi	Mal.
Judges	Judg.	Matthew	Matt.
Ruth	Ruth	Mark	Mark
1 Samuel	1 Sam.	Luke	Luke
2 Samuel	2 Sam.	John	John
1 Kings	1 Kings	Acts	Acts
2 Kings	2 Kings	Romans	Rom.
1 Chronicles	1 Chron.	1 Corinthians	1 Cor.
2 Chronicles	2 Chron.	2 Corinthians	2 Cor.
Ezra	Ezra	Galatians	Gal.
Nehemiah	Neh.	Ephesians	Eph.
Esther	Est.	Philippians	Phil.
Job	Job	Colossians	Col.
Psalms	Ps(s).	1 Thessalonians	1 Thess.
Proverbs	Prov.	2 Thessalonians	2 Thess.
Ecclesiastes	Eccl.	1 Timothy	1 Tim.
Song of Songs	Song	2 Timothy	2 Tim.
Isaiah	Isa.	Titus	Titus
Jeremiah	Jer.	Philemon	Philem.
Lamentations	Lam.	Hebrews	Heb.
Ezekiel	Ezek.	James	James
Daniel	Dan.	1 Peter	1 Peter
Hosea	Hos.	2 Peter	2 Peter
Joel	Joel	1 John	1 John
Amos	Amos	2 John	2 John
Obadiah	Obad.	3 John	3 John
Jonah	Jonah	Jude	Jude
Micah	Mic.	Revelation	Rev.

Sources

Acts

The question of sources for understanding the history of the early (New Testament) church is an important one, since not all scholars agree on the reliability of the information that is available. We need to state at the outset which sources we find acceptable.

One of the most important sources is the book of Acts (written by the same person as the third Gospel—presumably Luke). The author begins his story of the New Testament church with the outpouring of the Holy Spirit on Pentecost (ch. 2). He goes on to describe what happened to the first born-again believers in Jerusalem and how they eventually spread the gospel to other parts of the world. In particular he chronicles the missionary outreach of the apostle Peter until he departed for some unknown place (12:17). Then he follows the missionary work of Paul through three separate evangelistic journeys until he arrives in chains in Rome.

Many nonevangelical scholars discount Acts as a valid source for early church history. They maintain the author was far too biased to give an accurate account of what happened. Such scholars, of course, do not accept the inspiration of Scripture, which is a starting point of doctrine for this book. Because Luke was writing under the guidance of the Holy Spirit, he was not misshaping the history of the church but reporting accurately what took place.

It is true, of course, that Luke has a theological agenda in his book. He wants, for instance, to stress the tremendous power of the Holy Spirit, the love and unity of the early church, the legitimacy of the apostleship of Paul, and the fact that the early Christians were not revolutionaries but law-abiding citizens of the Roman Empire. Luke is therefore selective in what incidents he chooses to write about, but he is not inaccurate.

Furthermore, Luke is not exhaustive in his story of the outreach of the gospel. He says nothing about how the church developed in Arabia, Egypt, and areas east of Palestine. He does not even tell us when, how, and by whom the church in Rome was organized. His goal is to show, in an orderly and selective manner, how the gospel began in Jerusalem, then reached out to Judea and Samaria, and eventually spread far across the then-known world (1:8).

The New Testament Letters

Another important source of information for the history of the early church is the New Testament letters, particularly the letters of the apostle Paul. The so-called General Letters (Hebrews to Jude), while they do give us a general insight into the experiences and problems of the early church, give us little specific historical information. By and large we do not know for sure when these letters were written or to whom. The matter is different, of course, for the seven letters in Revelation 2–3, which give us specific information on churches in Asia Minor toward the end of the first century.

The thirteen letters written by the apostle Paul, however, are filled with information on what was going on in his personal life and in the lives of the churches he organized and served. While we cannot date with accuracy all of his letters (e.g., Galatians and Philippians), there is a general consensus, especially among evangelicals, when many of his letters were written and what specific situations the apostle was addressing. By and large we can link what Paul wrote in his letters with information contained in Acts, filling in some of the details that Luke omits. That is the approach we will be taking in this book.

It is not as if there are no problems in linking Acts and the Pauline letters. For example, when Paul writes about his second visit to Jerusalem in Galatians 2:1, is this the visit of Paul recorded in Acts 11:27–30 or in 15:1–29? Scholars are equally divided on this issue. If, as seems likely, Luke accompanied Paul on some of his journeys, why is there no reference to him until Colossians and Philemon (when Paul was a prisoner in Rome)? Or again, was Paul released from prison in Rome after Acts 28, as 2 Timothy 4:16–17 suggests, and if so, why does Luke make no reference to it or to any subsequent travels of Paul? We cannot answer with certainty any of these questions, but that should not stop us from using both Acts and the letters of Paul to give us at least some of the history of the early Christian church.

Other Written Sources

As far as we know, we have no other written sources on the history of the New Testament church contemporaneous with that period. We do have the Apostolic Fathers, who wrote in the second century (except for Clement's letter from Rome to the church in Corinth), but their writings are primarily hortatory and moral in nature. We also have the writings of Josephus, but for the most part (with the exception of a few comments on James the Just, whom he identifies as the brother of Jesus, who was called Christ) he says little about the development of Christianity; some of the specific references to Christ, his crucifixion under Pontius Pilate, and his reputed resurrection were most likely included by later Christian copyists, so that we can no longer know exactly what came from the pen of Josephus.

There were writers in the mid-to-late second or early third century who wrote about events that took place in the church—writers such as Papias, Hegesippus, Sextus Africanus—but none of their works are extant. We know about them only from Eusebius of Caesarea, a learned Christian who wrote in the late third and early fourth centuries.

Eusebius's *Church History* is the first known Christian attempt after Luke to give a chronological account of the history of the church from the life of Christ to his own time. He had access to a massive library in Caesarea, Palestine, where he was a research librarian. He collected and wrote down much of what he found on the first three hundred years of Christianity, citing almost 250 passages of various writers of antiquity. He relied heavily on Luke's writings, but he also preserved other traditions about the Christian community in Jerusalem and early Syriac Christianity, and he wrote anecdotes he found about the apostles in their service for the Lord.

The biggest difficulty with Eusebius's *Church History* is that he made no attempt to determine the historical value of what he wrote. Some of his data almost certainly are true, such as the fact that Peter eventually went to Rome, where he was martyred. But much is also legendary, such as how the grandchildren of Jude (Jesus' brother) together managed to put a stop to Domitian's persecution and then ruled the churches. We will occasionally refer to his work.

Archaeological Information

Another possible source for the history of the church is archaeology. We will not include here the highlights of how archaeology intersects with the historical data of the New Testament; that has been done in another book in this series, *Zondervan Quick Reference Library: Biblical Archaeology*. The introduction to that book discusses in greater detail the value of what has come to be known as *biblical archaeology*.

It stands to reason that we cannot expect to find much in the ruins of the Middle East that sheds additional light on what happened to Christians during the first century. After all, for the first two centuries at least, Christians met not in separate church buildings but in homes; we have no way of knowing, however, which homes may have served as house churches. Believers also met in synagogues, as the Scriptures suggest; there are ruins of first-century synagogues, but these give no evidence that there was ever a Christian presence in them. That is probably not to be expected, of course, since the early Christians were seen as a sect of Judaism and the earliest use of uniquely Christian symbols, such as the fish, anchor, and lamb, do not occur until about the end of the second century, and then only in cemeteries.

Some of the findings of archaeology do help at least to support the antiquity and reliability of the biblical data. For example, throughout much of the twentieth century, many scholars contested that the Gospel of John was a mid-to-late second-century document. But then p^{52} was found, a small fragment of a papyrus dated A.D. 125, which contained a tiny portion of this Gospel; this astounding discovery demonstrates beyond reasonable doubt that the Gospel of John, which is usually considered to be the last Gospel written, had to have been written no later than the late first century. In other words, in the Scriptures we have documents that were written by people who could have possibly known Christ and certainly the apostles.

Finally, there are a few classical sources, such as Tacitus's *Annals* (which has a section on Nero's persecution of Christians after the great fire of Rome), that help fill in certain gaps on what happened in the first-century church.

Pentecost and Outreach in Jerusalem

Prior to Pentecost

Just before Jesus ascended into heaven, he gave his followers both a promise and a challenge. His promise was that in a few days he was going to send to them the Holy Spirit, who would endue them with great spiritual power. Once that happened, they were to go out and be witnesses of all the things that they had seen Jesus do and say, beginning in Jerusalem, branching out into Judea and Samaria, and eventually reaching to the ends of the earth (Acts 1:8).

Thereupon, the followers of Jesus waited in Jerusalem in the upstairs room where they were staying—the total number being about 120, including both men and women (Acts 1:12–14). They spent much of their time together in intense prayer for the coming event, perhaps as a result of Jesus' instruction: "If you then, though you are evil, know how to give good gifts to your children, how much more will your Father in heaven give the Holy Spirit to those who ask him!" (Luke 11:13).

During the ten days before the outpouring of the Holy Spirit on Pentecost, the followers of Jesus did one other thing. Since the disciple Judas had defected from their group, betrayed the Lord into the hands of his enemies, and subsequently died by his own hand, the apostles felt it was important to appoint a replacement for him. The number twelve was significant, since these men were going to form the nucleus of a new people of God, comparable to the twelve tribes of Israel.

Therefore Simon Peter, who functioned as the group's leader, proposed that two men be selected who could fulfill the qualifications for being an apostle: one who had been with the Lord Jesus from the beginning of his ministry and who had been a witness of his resurrection (Acts 1:15–22). The two men nominated for this position were Joseph Barsabbas and Matthias. After the disciples had prayed, asking the Lord to select the right one, they cast lots between the two of them, and the lot fell on Matthias. Nothing more is known about him, however.

Pentecost

Ten days after Jesus had ascended into heaven, a most astounding event happened—one that rightfully has been called the birthday of the church. The 120 followers of Jesus were altogether in one place, when suddenly "a sound like the blowing of a violent wind came from heaven and filled the whole house where they were sitting" (Acts 2:2). At the same time tongues of fire appeared to rest on each person, and they were all filled with the Holy Spirit "and began to speak in other tongues as the Spirit enabled them" (2:4).

These phenomena were not imaginary or apparent only to the disciples of Jesus, since people throughout Jerusalem rushed to the scene to see what was going on. The crowd that gathered included not only residents of the city but also visitors from all over the Roman empire, who had come to the holy city for the Feast of Tabernacles. Some of the onlookers mocked what was going on, charging that it was simply a group of drunken Jews making a lot of commotion. But others were perplexed, since they were hearing words in their own languages from people who did not normally speak those languages.

Then Simon Peter, once again the spokesman for the group of Jesus' followers, stood up and addressed the crowd (Acts 2:14–36). He told them that this was the beginning of the fulfillment of the Old Testament prophecies for a mighty outpouring of the Holy Spirit in the last days. This was happening as a result of the promise of Jesus, the Messiah whom God had promised for centuries to send, who had fulfilled God's promises in the Scriptures through his ministry, cross, and resurrection, and who was now sitting at God's right hand as Lord of all. Peter charged the crowd with being responsible for the crucifixion of God's Messiah.

The people were smitten by Peter's message and asked what they should do. Peter instructed them to repent and be baptized in the name of Jesus, so that they might receive the forgiveness of their sins as well as the Holy Spirit as a gift. Peter received an amazing response to this call to salvation; on that one day alone, three thousand people were baptized and added to the church (2:37–41).

The New Christian Community

The Bible uses four words to describe the activities of the new community, centered around the apostles, that developed in this body of more than three thousand Spirit-filled Christians: *teaching*, *fellowship*, *breaking of bread*, and *prayer* (Acts 2:42).

Teaching. In his Pentecost sermon Peter had given a brief summary of what Jesus said and did. But much more needed to be taught to this new community of faith in order to shape their hearts and their lives. The responsibility for doing this fell on the apostles. The Lord had charged them with passing on all the important details of his ministry, death, and resurrection. Their teachings were eventually encapsulated in the four Gospels.

Fellowship. The new believers quickly formed a community of love. The haves among them were eager to share their possessions with the have-nots. Some among them even sold their "possessions and goods" in order to help out the less fortunate among them (Acts 2:45; 4:32–35). The apostles took charge of distributing food to the needy (cf. 6:1).

Breaking of bread. On a regular basis the new Christians broke bread together (2:46). This seems to refer not to the mere act of eating a meal together, but to a special way of remembering the Lord Jesus. Perhaps they were reenacting what had taken place in the upper room before Jesus went to Gethsemane; perhaps they were recalling how Jesus had broken bread with them and eaten after he was raised from the dead (cf. Luke 24:30, 35, 41–42; Acts 1:4). In any case, this special commemoration eventually became the Eucharist.

Prayer. The early Christians had regular times of worship, including especially prayer. Every day they went to the temple courts to praise God's name, to thank him for miracles being performed in the name of Jesus, and to pray for one another. According to Luke, nothing important in the history of the New Testament church happened outside a context of prayer.

Life in this new community of faith was exciting and contagious. People living in Jerusalem could not help but notice what was happening, and every day more were accepting Jesus as the Messiah. Within a short time their numbers climbed to five thousand men, besides women and children (4:4).

Miracles of the Apostles

One of the things that attracted large audiences to listen to the Christian message was "wonders and miraculous signs" done through the hands of the apostles, which filled people with awe (Acts 2:43). Luke records an example of how this worked in Acts 3.

One day Peter and John were going into the temple to pray, as they often did. Sitting at one of the gates of the temple was a fortysome-year-old man who had been crippled from birth (Acts 4:22). He was begging for money from those going into the temple, for one of the key elements in Judaism was the giving of alms. When Peter saw the deformed man, he told him to look at him and John. The man did so, expecting to receive a large handout. Then Peter said: "Silver or gold I do not have, but what I have I give you. In the name of Jesus Christ of Nazareth, walk." He grabbed the man's right hand and helped him to his feet.

Immediately the man's legs became strong. He jumped up and accompanied Peter and John into the temple, leaping and praising God. All this unusual commotion in the temple attracted the attention of the other worshipers, and they recognized who this man was. They came running to the part of the temple known as Solomon's Colonnade, and when a large crowd had gathered, Peter used the opportunity to preach the gospel to the people.

In his message, Peter insisted that he and John had not done anything in their own power; rather, it was only by the power of Jesus of Nazareth that the crippled man had been healed. The apostle then reviewed the life, ministry, death, and resurrection of Jesus, as he had done on Pentecost. He closed his message with a call for the people to repent of their sins and turn to the Lord Jesus as God's promised Messiah. In this case, Peter referred to Deuteronomy 18:15–19, the passage in which it was prophesied that the Coming One would be a great prophet like Moses.

Many of those who listened to Peter and John put their faith in Jesus as the Messiah as a result of this miraculous healing and Peter's follow-up sermon. But to the Jewish religious leaders, the apostles were becoming a threat. They seized Peter and John and put them in jail overnight, planning to interrogate them the following morning.

Before the Jewish Authorities

The next day the Jewish Sanhedrin convened and had Peter and John brought before them for questioning: "By what power or what name did you [heal the crippled man]?" they asked (Acts 4:7). Standing with them was that same crippled man (4:14)

Only a couple months earlier, Peter had been so terrified of what might happen to him if the Jews knew he was associated with Jesus that he denied three times he had ever known Jesus. But now, filled with the Holy Spirit, Peter confronted the "rulers and elders of the people" with the claims of Jesus, insisting that salvation could be found in no other name besides Jesus (4:8–12).

The Sanhedrin was now confronted with a real dilemma. They could not deny that a great miracle had been done; at the same time, they did not want the message about Jesus as the Messiah to spread any further. So after they had conferred without Peter and John in their midst, they summoned them back into the room and ordered them to stop speaking about Jesus. Once again, fearless Peter spoke up, telling the chief priests and teachers of the law that they had no choice but to speak "about what [they had] seen and heard" (4:20). The authorities issued further threats against the two apostles, then let them go.

Peter and John went back to their own people and told them what had happened and what the Sanhedrin had said. Undoubtedly, some among the Christian community must have felt fear rise within their hearts; after all, speaking about Jesus was now against the law. They knew they needed strength from the Lord Jesus and his Spirit to continue the mission he had given them. They therefore spent some time in intense prayer, asking the Lord to continue to give them boldness to preach in the face of these threats (4:23–30). They recognized that they were facing a situation not unlike that which Jesus had faced throughout his life.

When they had finished praying, God gave them a fresh filling of his Holy Spirit, and they "spoke the word of God boldly" (4:31). They continued to meet as a group in Solomon's Colonnade, where they performed miracles and told others about Jesus (5:12–16). Their numbers continued to grow.

Problems Within and Without

Though the church was young and dynamic, it was not without its problems. People carried into the church their sinful nature. One married couple, Ananias and Sapphira, noticed the positive attention that a man named Joseph Barnabas received from selling some property and bringing the money to the apostles (Acts 4:36–37), and they wanted this same attention. So they also sold some of their property and brought the money to the apostles, but they conspired together to keep part of it back for themselves.

The Holy Spirit showed Peter what was going on in the hearts of this couple, and he confronted them separately. He told them that what concerned the Lord most was not their keeping part of the money; giving money, after all, was voluntary, not mandatory. Rather, it was their attempt to deceive the church and its Lord. When Ananias and Sapphira heard these words, both "fell down and died" (5:5, 10). Naturally, "great fear seized the whole church" (v. 11).

As the apostles continued to preach, heal people, and cast out demons, the Jewish authorities again arrested them and jailed them overnight. This time an angel of the Lord came to the apostles in the prison and released them, and they reentered the temple the next day to continue preaching. The Sanhedrin convened the next day, and when someone told them that the apostles were out preaching again, they sent the temple guard to bring them in for questioning.

As before, Peter fearlessly insisted they would obey God rather than human authorities, and he again outlined the injustice they had done to Jesus (5:29–32). Some in the room became so furious that they wanted to kill the apostles. But a prominent Pharisee named Gamaliel stood up and cautioned restraint: "If their purpose or activity is of human origin, it will fail. But if it is from God, you will not be able to stop these men" (5:38–39).

Gamaliel's words prevailed. The authorities called the apostles back into the room. This time they not only ordered them to stop talking about Jesus, but they also gave them a flogging. The apostles, however, returned to their people, "rejoicing because they had been counted worthy of suffering disgrace for the Name [of Jesus]" (v. 41). They kept on spreading the word.

Stephen and Philip and Outreach in Judea and Samaria

The Choosing of the Seven

Success, especially rapid success, usually brings unanticipated problems. Thus it was with the church in the New Testament. When it had grown to over five thousand people, internal problems began to surface.

In the Roman world, Jews lived and worked in every part of the empire. But they always had an attachment to Jerusalem as the center of their faith. Occasionally they would go to the holy city to attend one of the annual feasts, especially Passover, and many elderly Jews chose to retire in Jerusalem, so that they could be buried there. Jews who spent most of their lives outside Palestine were called Hellenistic Jews.

Many Hellenistic Jews were among those who came to believe in Jesus as the Messiah as a result of the apostles' preaching. Since, like today, women tended to outlive their husbands, many of them were widows. Widows at that time had few financial resources of their own, and Christian widows of both Hebraic and Hellenistic background had to depend on the charity of the church for their sustenance. A problem developed, for the Hellenistic widows felt that they "were being overlooked in the daily distribution of food" (Acts 6:1).

Something had to be done to quell this dissent. Because the church had grown so large and the work was so demanding, the apostles realized that they could no longer manage all aspects of its life. They also knew that God had especially gifted them with "the ministry of the word of God" (6:2). Thus, they proposed that other people who were uniquely gifted in ministering to the needy be appointed. The apostles would turn over that responsibility to them.

This suggestion pleased everyone, and seven men filled with the Holy Spirit and wisdom were selected: Stephen, Philip, Procorus, Nicanor, Timon, Parmenas, and Nicholas. These men were presented to the apostles, who prayed for them and laid their hands on them. The grumbling concerning the care of the needy apparently ceased, and the word of God continued to spread.

Stephen's Ministry

Stephen, one of the Seven commissioned to help with the daily distribution of food to the needy, discovered he had other gifts as well. He had received the gifts of doing "great wonders and miraculous signs" and of defending the gospel of Christ against its detractors.

Opposition to Christianity arose particularly in one of the Hellenistic synagogues in Jerusalem, called the Synagogue of the Freedmen. So powerful was the defense of Stephen, himself a Hellenistic Jewish Christian, that no one was able to withstand his wisdom and insight. He particularly pointed out, on the basis of many stories in the Old Testament, that God could be worshiped everywhere and that he had never intended his residence to be limited to the temple in Jerusalem. With the coming of Jesus Christ, God now wanted his message of salvation to go out freely to all people, to the ends of the earth.

Since the Jews were unable to refute Stephen's arguments, they did the next best thing. They hauled him in front of the Sanhedrin, together with false witnesses who insisted they heard Stephen say that Jesus of Nazareth (and presumably also, then, the Christian community) was going to destroy the temple and sacred Jewish customs.

The Sanhedrin gave Stephen the opportunity to defend himself. Acts 7 records his speech, in which he not only powerfully defended his message, but also showed them how, throughout Israel's history, the religious establishment consistently rejected the true message of God revealed through the prophets, the last of whom was the great Prophet, Jesus. In fact, they had even murdered him, "the Righteous One" (7:51–52).

Stephen's speech infuriated the Jewish authorities, and they railed against him. Stephen then reported a vision of Jesus, standing at God's right hand. The authorities could take it no longer. They did not even wait for an official verdict; instead, they rushed at Stephen and dragged him outside the city, where they stoned him to death. Stephen was thus the first martyr for the cause of Christ. Luke mentions one person in particular as approving of his death—a young man by the name of Saul.

The Spread of the Gospel

After the martyrdom of Stephen, the Sanhedrin instituted an all-out persecution of the church in Jerusalem, particularly aimed at Christians who believed as Stephen did. One of the key Jewish figures who put believers in prison was Saul (see Acts 8:3; Gal. 1:13–14; 1 Tim. 1:13). Apparently those who kept themselves within the context of law-abiding Judaism did not suffer persecution; at least, Luke reports that "the apostles" were able to remain in Jerusalem (Acts 8:1) without being harmed.

Since it was now becoming dangerous to be a Christian, many decided to flee the holy city and live elsewhere, either in Judea or in Samaria. But rather than stifling the new movement, this organized persecution actually aided its spread. The believers who fled did not keep silent about their newfound faith; they told everyone everywhere about Jesus. Through what we might now call "lay evangelism," new groups of Christians began to crop up all over Palestine.

This spread of the gospel by laypeople was not limited to the Christians who had just fled Jerusalem. Even though Luke does not record it in Acts, there apparently was a general tendency for any new believers to talk about Jesus wherever they went and to organize into Christian communities. For example, we know that Christianity spread to the city of Rome. When the apostle Paul addressed a letter to the Romans at the end of his third missionary journey, he was writing to a group of believers in Rome. Moreover, when, two years later, he actually arrived in Rome as a prisoner, he was met by numerous Christians from the capital city of the empire (see Acts 28:14–15). There was a similar Christian group in Puteoli (28:14).

We have no record, either in Scripture or in church tradition, of any apostle starting these churches. The most reasonable explanation is that they were started by believers who had been in Jerusalem on the Day of Pentecost and who were among the three thousand who accepted Jesus as their Savior and Lord that day. When they returned home, they began to tell others what had happened in Jerusalem and what Jesus had done during his life and ministry as Israel's Messiah and the Savior of the world.

Philip Preaches in Samaria

Philip, one of the Seven appointed to help with the daily distribution of food (Acts 6), discovered, like Stephen, that in addition to his gift of waiting at tables, he also had the gifts of evangelism and performing miracles (see Acts 8:5–8; 21:8). During the persecution following Stephen's martyrdom, he settled in Caesarea (8:40).

Until now, all evangelism had been limited to Jews—either Hebraic Jews or Hellenistic Jews. But Philip decided to try something different. Perhaps taking his cue from Jesus himself (see John 4), he began to evangelize a city in Samaria. The Samaritans were what we might call half-breed Jews: Ethnically, this race was most likely formed from the remnant left in Palestine after the Israelites had been deported by the Assyrians and the Jews taken into exile to Babylon; they intermarried with other races who had settled in that region. The Samaritans believed the Jewish Scriptures (particularly the Pentateuch), but did not think that the temple in Jerusalem was the place where God had to be worshiped (John 4:20). Jews tended to avoid these people.

Philip was highly successful in his evangelism of the Samaritans. When Peter and John heard about the spread of the gospel in this region, they decided to investigate. They noticed that for some reason, the Samaritans had not received the full power of the Holy Spirit when they believed and were baptized. So the two apostles placed their hands on the new believers, who then received the Holy Spirit.

Among those converted by Philip's preaching was a man named Simon, who had had a career as a prominent magician, or sorcerer. When he saw the evidence of the power of the Holy Spirit communicated by Peter and John, he wanted the ability to bestow this power and offered the apostles money. But the ability to give the Holy Spirit cannot be bought or sold. Peter therefore spoke harsh words of judgment against Simon and instructed him to repent of his sin.

Peter and John stayed for some days in Samaria and proclaimed the word of God. Seeing that God had also given his Holy Spirit to these semi-Jews, as the apostles made their way back to Jerusalem, they evangelized many other villages in Samaria.

Philip and the Ethiopian Eunuch

One day as Philip was going about evangelizing, an angel appeared to him and directed him to go to a deserted highway that led from Jerusalem to the Gaza strip. He may have thought this was an odd place to be sent, but Philip obeyed the angel.

As he traveled along that road, off in the distance he saw a man riding in a chariot. This man was a eunuch from the country of Ethiopia, where he served as a treasurer in the court of his queen, Candace. He had gone to Jerusalem to worship; presumably, he was either a proselyte to Judaism or a God-fearer (someone interested in the Jewish religion, but unwilling to undergo circumcision in order to become a full Jew), a Gentile by birth, since no law-abiding Jew would undergo the surgery necessary to become a eunuch (cf. Deut. 23:1).

As he was riding along in his chariot, the Ethiopian was reading aloud from Isaiah 53, one of the servant songs of Isaiah. The Spirit directed Philip to go near the chariot, and when he heard what the man was reading, he asked, "Do you understand what you are reading?" (Acts 8:30). The eunuch then invited Philip into his chariot to explain to him the message of the prophet. Philip took the opportunity to point out how the suffering servant in Isaiah 53 was prophetic of Jesus Christ, the Lamb of God who takes away the sin of the world (Acts 8:32–35).

As Philip explained the message of the Scriptures and its fulfillment in Jesus Christ, the Holy Spirit began to work in the Ethiopian's heart, and he became a believer. As they passed a small oasis along that desert road, the Ethiopian asked Philip if he might be baptized. Philip was glad to comply, and he baptized the eunuch into the name of Jesus (8:36–38). Philip's task was now completed, so the Spirit directed him to go northwest in the Gaza strip to Azotus (the old Philistine city of Ashdod), where he continued to evangelize.

The Ethiopian eunuch headed south toward Ethiopia with his newfound faith in his heart. According to church tradition (see Eusebius, *Church History*, 2.1), he shared his knowledge of God and salvation in the name of Jesus with others in his country and helped to establish a Christian community there.

Peter and the Winds of Change

Peter As Missionary in Judea

Up to this time, Peter had remained with the other apostles in Jerusalem, where he had functioned as one of the main leaders in the church. Just as he had earlier gone with John to visit the new Christians in Samaria (Acts 8:14–25), he decided to visit some of the new Christians elsewhere in Judea—those who had become Christians as a result of the lay evangelizing that took place after the martyrdom of Stephen.

One of the first towns Peter visited was Lydda, about thirty miles along a road to the northwest of Jerusalem. There someone informed him about a paralytic named Aeneas, who had been bedridden for eight years. Peter visited this man and healed him in the name of Jesus. When people heard about the miracle, many turned to the Lord (Acts 9:32–35).

Peter continued traveling along the same road, which led toward the Mediterranean Sea, and arrived in Joppa, a coastal city (modern Jaffa). Some believers told him about a dear elderly Christian woman named Dorcas, a seamstress who had done many deeds of kindness for poor widows. She had recently become sick and had died, and they begged Peter to come. The apostle went to an upstairs room where Dorcas was lying. He sent the people out of the room and, through the power of prayer and the Holy Spirit, called her back to life. Once again, this miracle had an amazing impact on the people of that town; many put their faith in Jesus (9:36–42).

For some reason—perhaps because the persecution led by Saul was intensifying—Peter decided not to return immediately to Jerusalem. Instead, he took up residence in Joppa, in the house of Simon, a tanner. Presumably he continued to minister to the new believers there and to evangelize the Jews.

Peter's Vision in Joppa

One day at noon, Peter was hungry. While he was waiting for lunch to be prepared, he went on the roof of Simon's house to pray; as he did so, he fell into a trance. In his vision, he saw a sheet being let down from heaven by its four corners. In the sheet were all sorts of clean and unclean animals and birds, including reptiles. Many of these were on the list of foods that Jews were forbidden to eat (see Lev. 11). Then Peter heard a voice from heaven that instructed him to kill these animals and eat them. Peter vigorously objected to this command.

The heavenly voice came a second time: "Do not call anything impure that God has made clean" (Acts 10:15). Three times this happened; then the vision was over.

Such a strange vision puzzled Peter: What did it mean? At precisely that moment, three men were knocking at the door of Simon's house. They had come from Caesarea, thirty miles north of Joppa, also on the coast of the Mediterranean Sea. They were Gentiles, and they had been sent there by a Roman centurion named Cornelius.

Cornelius was a God-fearing Gentile, who prayed to the God of the Jews and regularly aided the poor, though he never officially became a Jew. The previous afternoon he had received a visit from an angel, who told him to send men to Joppa, to the house of Simon the tanner, and to ask for Simon Peter (10:1–8). The three men he sent were the ones knocking at Simon's door.

Peter had never had close associations with Gentiles or eaten with them. Suddenly he realized the meaning of his vision. God was telling him that such people could no longer be considered "untouchables," because God was accepting them as people who needed to hear the gospel (cf. 10:28). Peter invited the men into the house to be his guests, and the following day he went with them to Caesarea, accompanied by six other believers from Joppa (cf. 11:12).

Uncircumcised Gentiles Become Believers

When Peter arrived at Cornelius's house in Caesarea, he found a large group of Gentiles, all relatives and friends of the centurion, gathered there. Peter reported God's revelation of the previous day that he should associate with Gentiles, and then he asked why he had been summoned.

Cornelius responded with the story of his visit from an angel. Since Simon Peter was now in their midst, the centurion said, "Now we are all here in the presence of God to listen to everything the Lord has commanded you to tell us" (Acts 10:33). Peter then began to tell his attentive audience all about Jesus—his healing and teaching ministry, his crucifixion, and his resurrection. Since Cornelius was familiar with the Old Testament, Peter showed how many Old Testament prophecies had predicted the events of Jesus' life. He closed with a call for people to believe in Jesus in order to receive the forgiveness of sins and the gift of salvation.

An amazing thing then happened: The Holy Spirit of the Lord suddenly descended on this group of people, and they began to speak in tongues (10:44–46). Peter recognized that this could only mean that these people had received the Lord Jesus in their hearts as Savior. Therefore, nothing should prevent them from being baptized. The Christians who had accompanied Peter agreed, and Peter baptized them into the name of Jesus.

This was the first time that uncircumcised Gentiles had been accepted by Jews as members of God's covenant people. It had taken the indisputable, dramatic event of the outpouring of the Holy Spirit on them to convince Peter that God now made no distinction between Jews and Gentiles.

Peter's dealings with these Gentiles, however, did not go over so well when news of what he had done reached the believers in Jerusalem. They therefore called for him to explain his actions (Acts 11:1–17). Accompanied by those who had witnessed the event, he reported what had happened. The leaders in Jerusalem accepted this explanation and praised God that now even the uncircumcised could become Christians without first becoming Jews.

Peter's Miraculous Release From Prison

It was now several years since Jesus had ascended into heaven and poured out his Spirit. Churches had sprung up in many cities of the Roman Empire, and their members came mainly from among the Jews. In a few localities, however, such as Antioch in Syria, Gentiles were also admitted into the church (Acts 11:20–21).

Politically, Palestine was ruled by Herod Agrippa I, the grandson of Herod the Great. Through a series of shrewd political maneuvers, including a long-time friendship with the new Roman emperor, Caligula, Agrippa had managed to become king of the entire area over which his grandfather had ruled. He moved his capital to Jerusalem and did some major repair on the northern wall of the holy city in an attempt to endear himself to the Jews.

For the most part, the Jews hated being ruled by any of the Herodians. Most of those who had ended up in positions of power were cruel despots. Thus, Herod Agrippa was determined to do whatever was necessary to gain the favor of the Jews. Part of this included the suppression of minorities—including Christians. He had a number of them arrested and put in prison, and he executed James, the brother of John son of Zebedee (12:2). When he saw how pleased the majority of the Jews were, he decided to continue the practice.

About that time Peter returned to Jerusalem to celebrate the Passover. When Agrippa noticed that another key Christian leader was in town, he had him arrested and locked in the inner part of the prison, fully intending to have him beheaded after the Feast. But the church members held all-night prayer vigils on Peter's behalf.

The night before Peter's scheduled execution, an angel from the Lord suddenly woke him up and told him to follow him. Peter's chains fell off, and the prison doors miraculously opened. Peter wasn't sure if he was asleep or awake, but when the angel left him outside the prison walls, he knew it was real. He headed for the home of the mother of John Mark, where one of the prayer meetings was taking place. Peter knocked at the gate. A servant girl, Rhoda, ran to the gate and back to the group, announcing Peter was there. They told her she was only imagining things, but she insisted it was true.

Peter kept knocking. After the believers realized that it was really Peter knocking at the gate, they let him in and praised the God who had so marvelously delivered him.

Peter and "Another Place"

After Peter, upon his release from prison, had greeted the believers praying for him in the home of John Mark, we read that, still under cover of night, "he left for another place" (Acts 12:17). Where did he go and what did he do?

Most likely Peter did not return to Joppa, for that was still territory under King Herod Agrippa's jurisdiction. Even though Agrippa killed the prison guards who had "let" Peter escape, he would surely have rearrested the apostle on the spot if he found him anywhere in his kingdom. That danger, however, did not last too long, because shortly after this incident Herod was suddenly killed by divine intervention (Acts 12:19b–23).

Peter apparently now began to do missionary work (cf. 1 Cor. 9:5). Even though he had accepted the legitimacy of mission work among the Gentiles, he concentrated his efforts on winning Jews to Christ (see Gal. 2:7–9). Where? When he wrote his first letter, he addressed it to "God's elect, strangers in the world, scattered throughout Pontus, Galatia, Cappadocia, Asia and Bithynia" (1 Peter 1:1)—the northern part of Asia Minor, immediately south of the Black Sea (present-day northern Turkey). His addressing believers in this area and his familiarity with their situation suggest that Peter spent at least some of his time evangelizing that region.

Paul's reference to a "Peter party" in Corinth (1 Cor. 1:12; "Cephas" is the Aramaic word for "Peter") suggests the possibility that he spent some time in that city in the mid-50s. We also find Peter in Jerusalem in A.D. 52, taking a leading role at the Council of Jerusalem, where an official decision had to be made whether Gentiles who became believers had to be circumcised (Acts 15:7–11). By that time, the leadership of the church in Jerusalem had passed to James, the brother of Jesus (cf. Acts 15:13–21; 21:18; Gal. 1:19; 2:9, 12). Peter also spent some time in Antioch, where he had a confrontation with the apostle Paul over associating with Gentiles (Gal. 2:11–14).

Church tradition is unanimous that in the later years of his life, Peter moved to Rome, though there is no evidence that he served as "bishop of Rome" for twenty-five years, as some traditions claim. When the Roman emperor Nero began persecuting Christians after the burning of Rome (in the mid-60s), Peter was apparently crucified (cf. John 21:18–19).

Paul—Conversion to
First Missionary Journey

From Saul the Persecutor to Paul, the Called Apostle

The persecution of Christians in Judea was spearheaded by an energetic and zealous Pharisee named Saul. He spared no effort to enter synagogues, find out who were believers, arrest them, and imprison them in Jerusalem. Apparently he had run out of synagogues in Judea, so he asked for and received authorization from the high priest to carry out his "murderous threats" in other cities, such as Damascus (Acts 9:1–2; 26:10–11).

As Saul was nearing Damascus about noon, suddenly a bright light from heaven flashed around him and a voice called out, "Saul, Saul, why do you persecute me? It is hard for you to kick against the goads" (9:4; 22:7; 26:14). Saul was shocked, for he was positive he had been doing the work of the Lord. Thus, he responded, "Who are you, Lord?" The voice then identified himself as the Lord Jesus and told him to go into Damascus to await further orders.

When Saul got up from the ground, he discovered he could not see, so he asked his companions to lead him into Damascus. They dropped him off at the house of Judas on Straight Street. There Saul fasted for three days, spending his time in intense prayer and inner reflection on this experience and on what he had been doing in his life to this point.

The Lord then appeared to a Christian disciple named Ananias, instructing him to find Saul, lay his hands on him, and restore his sight. Understandably Ananias balked, for he had heard about Saul's reputation. But the Lord assured him that Saul was a changed man. In fact, the Lord told Ananias that this man was to be his "chosen instrument to carry [his] name before the Gentiles" (9:15; cf. Gal. 1:15).

Ananias therefore obeyed the Lord. He found the designated house in which Saul was staying. He laid his hands on the chastened Pharisee, restored his sight, and instructed him to repent of his sins, call on the name of the Lord, be baptized, and receive the Holy Spirit (Acts 9:17; 22:14–16). Immediately something like scales fell from Saul's eyes, and he could see again. He was then baptized as a new believer and took some food, thus regaining his strength. God now had work for him to do in his kingdom.

Saul's First Days in Ministry for Jesus

The first thing Saul did after believing in Jesus and being baptized was to seek out other believers in Damascus. Within a few days, he was preaching in the synagogues of that city that Jesus was God's promised Messiah—the very synagogues in which he had hoped to arrest Christians (Acts 9:20). People were shocked, for everyone seemed to know why Saul had come to Damascus.

Saul needed time to sort some things through, so shortly after his conversion he spent up to three years in the northern Arabian desert near Damascus (Gal. 1:17). This was an area ruled by the Nabatean King Aretas. It may have been during this period that he received his vision in which he was caught up into the third heaven (2 Cor. 12:1–6), though most date this event later. Perhaps Saul did some evangelizing of the Nabateans, though we have no record of it. He then returned to Damascus.

Saul was an extremely knowledgeable Pharisee; he knew the Hebrew Scriptures thoroughly. All of this knowledge he now put to use as he argued in the synagogues of Damascus that Jesus was the Christ, the one who fulfilled the hope of Israel. His messages may even have sounded like that of Stephen in Acts 7. (Saul may have been one of the Jews from Cilicia who had debated Stephen [Acts 6:9–10].) Saul angered the Jews in Damascus so much that they conspired to kill him (9:23)! They kept watch day and night at the city gates for Saul's entrance into or exit from the city. Apparently they had an official warrant for his arrest from the governor of the city, an appointee of King Aretas (2 Cor. 11:32).

Someone tipped Saul off as to what might happen to him, so the Christians hid him somewhere in the city. One night, they lowered Saul in a basket from a window in the city wall (Acts 9:25; 2 Cor. 11:33), and he escaped. From there he returned to Jerusalem, nearly three years after he had left with the intention of destroying the church.

Saul Back in Judea

Part of Saul's goal of traveling to Jerusalem at this time was to meet with the apostles and discuss his theology with them—not to get their approval, but simply to share what he had been doing and thinking. Only two apostles were available: Peter and James, the brother of Jesus (Gal. 1:18–19). Saul also wanted to do some preaching in the synagogues of Jerusalem.

But Saul faced a problem: None of the followers of Jesus in Jerusalem would believe that he was really a changed man. They were sure that he was only pretending to be a believer in order to find out who the followers of Christ in Jerusalem were and then have them arrested. Barnabas, however, stood up for Saul and assured both the apostles and the believers that Saul's conversion was for real (Acts 9:26–27). Barnabas had apparently been in Damascus during part of Saul's stay there.

Saul remained in Jerusalem for only fifteen days (Gal. 1:18). Once the genuineness of his conversion had been established, he freely moved about in the synagogues of Jerusalem, preaching "boldly in the name of the Lord" (Acts 9:28). Like Stephen, he concentrated his efforts on Hellenistic Jews, and the reaction to him was the same as to Stephen: They wanted to kill him.

One day at the end of his stay in Jerusalem, Saul went to the temple to pray, where he fell into a trance. There the Lord told him specifically that his witness for Jesus would not be accepted in Jerusalem and that he was to leave the city and start preaching to Gentiles (Acts 22:17–21). This confirmed what Ananias had perhaps told him about God's plan for him (9:15–19).

When the Christian brothers in Jerusalem learned about the plot against Saul's life, they quickly took him down to Caesarea, put him on a ship, and sent him off to Tarsus in Cilicia, the city of his birth (Acts 9:30; cf. 22:3). The next few years are known as Saul's "silent years," since Luke does not talk about them, nor does Paul in his letters.

Pauline Chronology and the Silent Years

It appears as if Saul became a believer in Jesus in about A.D. 35 (only two years after Jesus' ascension into heaven). Saul's first visit to Jerusalem was, therefore, in about A.D. 38. His next visit to Jerusalem was the so-called famine visit (Acts 11:27–30), which occurred during the reign of Claudius (A.D. 41–54). That specific visit probably occurred sometime in the mid-40s, which means that from about A.D. 38 to 44, we know only something about Saul's whereabouts but precious little about his activities. (And at some point, perhaps during this time, Saul took as his preferred name Paul, the name by which he is known in his letters—see Acts 13:9.)

We get hints in Paul's letters, however, as to what happened to him during those eight years. In Galatians 1:21, Paul writes that after his first visit to Jerusalem, he spent his time in Syria and Cilicia. These two Roman provinces adjoined each other, along the eastern and northeastern coast of the Mediterranean Sea (present-day Lebanon, Syria, and eastern Turkey).

Jews lived and worked in numerous cities in these provinces, such as Tarsus, Issus, Seleucia, Antioch, and Damascus. Since by this time Saul had become a powerful spokesman for the gospel of Jesus, it is safe to assume that he spent as much time as he could preaching in the synagogues in these cities and evangelizing Gentiles. During these years he was also thinking through and developing his theology of salvation by grace alone. Furthermore, since he was a leather worker (cf. Acts 18:1–3) and insisted on working for his own living (1 Thess. 2:9; 2 Thess. 3:7–9), he certainly spent much of his time working at his trade.

In 2 Corinthians 11:23–27 the apostle Paul catalogues numerous sufferings he endured for the sake of the gospel from the time of his conversion to about A.D. 56 (when he wrote this letter). Some of these events are recorded in the book of Acts, but many are not. For example, he refers to five floggings he received from the Jews (Acts records none) and three shipwrecks he experienced (the one recorded in Acts 27 was his fourth shipwreck, occurring about A.D. 59). Some of these sufferings may have occurred during his first two missionary journeys, but certainly many of them also occurred during these silent years.

To Antioch and to Jerusalem a Second Time

In the early 40s, the preaching of the gospel was still by and large confined to Jews. Saul, of course, was probably by this time evangelizing Gentiles in obedience to the Lord's command, and Peter had had the vision recorded in Acts 10 and had preached to Cornelius and his family. But a general trend of trying to reach the uncircumcised with the gospel had not yet begun.

Some believers from Cyprus (an island in the Mediterranean) and Cyrene (a Roman province in Africa, west of Egypt), however, went to Antioch of Syria and started a regular practice of evangelizing uncircumcised Gentiles. They were successful in their preaching so that "a great number of people believed and turned to the Lord" (Acts 11:19–21).

News of what was happening in Antioch reached the church in Jerusalem, and the believers there wanted to know firsthand what was going on. They therefore decided to send someone to investigate and chose Barnabas, a trusted and Spirit-filled representative. When he arrived in Antioch and saw how God's grace was working in the hearts of Gentiles who had become believers, he became excited and "encouraged them all to remain true to the Lord with all their hearts" (11:23).

In fact, Barnabas seemed so convinced that this sort of evangelism was appropriate that he sent to Cilicia for Saul to come and help out. Presumably he chose Saul because he was aware that Saul knew better than anyone else how to approach Gentiles with the gospel in an effective manner. For a whole year the two of them stayed and worked in Antioch, greatly increasing the size of the church (11:25–26).

Toward the end of that year, sometime in A.D. 46, Palestine experienced a bad harvest and an ensuing famine. The Christians in Antioch wanted to help their fellow believers in Jerusalem, which seemed to be the hardest-hit area, and so they took up a love offering for them. They then sent their gift to the elders in that church via Barnabas and Saul (11:27–30). It is possible, though not certain, that this is the same visit Paul describes in Galatians 2:1–10.

Barnabas and Saul Leave on a Missionary Journey

Barnabas and Saul returned from their mission in Jerusalem and resumed their work in the church of Antioch in Syria. In the spring of A.D. 48, the Holy Spirit spoke to some prophets and teachers in that church, after a time of fasting and prayer, that he wanted Barnabas and Saul officially commissioned as missionaries, to go to other parts of the Roman world with the gospel (Acts 13:1–3). These prophets and teachers, therefore, laid their hands on the two chosen men and sent them off. Accompanying Barnabas and Saul was a cousin of Barnabas named John Mark (13:5; cf. Col. 4:10).

They headed for Seleucia, the port city connected with Antioch. There they embarked on a ship and sailed on the Mediterranean to the island of Cyprus, where Barnabas had grown up (Acts 4:36). They landed at Salamis on the eastern edge and traversed the entire island, establishing a pattern of always beginning their evangelism in a new city with the Jewish synagogue. At the opposite end of Cyprus was Paphos, the provincial capital.

The Roman proconsul of Cyprus was Sergius Paulus. Perhaps the preaching of Barnabas and Saul had created a certain amount of furor among the Jews of Cyprus, as it had already done elsewhere (cf. 9:22–23, 28–29), and Sergius needed to hear for himself what was going on. So he summoned the missionaries into his presence in order to make an independent judgment concerning the message they were preaching.

Surprisingly, perhaps, Barnabas and Saul received a sympathetic hearing from the Roman official. But a Jewish sorcerer named Bar-Jesus, one of the proconsul's attendants and perhaps advisers, tried to persuade him that the message he was hearing was dead wrong. Saul (now called Paul) looked Bar-Jesus straight in the eye, called him "a child of the devil," and pronounced temporary blindness on him (13:8–11). Paul's word immediately came true. Sergius Paulus was so impressed with his message and demonstration of spiritual power that he became a believer.

In Pamphylia and Galatia

Paul was never one to stay very long in the same place, so after his and Barnabas's whirlwind trip through Cyprus, they boarded a ship and headed for the coast of Asia Minor, landing at the port city of Perga (in the Roman province of Pamphylia). For some reason that Luke does not disclose, John Mark left the mission party there and returned to Jerusalem.

Paul and Barnabas immediately headed north inland and arrived in Antioch of Pisidia, part of the Roman province of Galatia. As they had done in Cyprus, they attended the synagogue in that city on the Sabbath and were invited, as visiting rabbis, to speak to those gathered. A summary of Paul's sermon is given in Acts 13:16–41; it bears strong similarities to Stephen's message in Acts 7. Paul closed with an encouragement to those gathered to believe in Jesus for the forgiveness of their sins, and a prophetic warning that if they did not believe, they would receive divine judgment.

The Jews were impressed with his message and invited Paul and Barnabas to preach the next Sabbath as well. But it appears that during the week, Paul also invited Gentiles to attend the service, because on the next Sabbath, "almost the whole city gathered to hear the word of the Lord" (13:44). This disturbed the Jews, who were not used to seeing their synagogue filled with Gentiles. Furthermore, it became apparent that Paul was going to invite them to become God's people without first undergoing Jewish initiation rights, such as circumcision.

Paul and Barnabas did not back off. Rather, they told the Jews that if they were going to reject the gospel, the two of them would continue to proclaim God's truth to the Gentiles, in fulfillment of God's promise in the Old Testament that his people were to be a light to the Gentiles (13:47; cf. Isa. 49:6). Paul's pattern of "first for the Jew, then for the Gentile" (Rom. 1:16) was now becoming firmly set. Many Gentiles in that region turned to the Lord.

The anger of the Jews grew to a boiling point, and they put pressure on the city magistrates, through their God-fearing (Gentile) wives, to do something about these troublemakers. What form of "persecution" the missionaries experienced is not spelled out, but they quickly left the city for other parts of Galatia (Acts 13:50–51).

Iconium and Lystra

From Antioch in Pisidia, Paul and Barnabas headed eighty miles southeast to the city of Iconium, still in the province of Galatia. Once again, Paul and Barnabas headed for the Jewish synagogue on the Sabbath and were invited to speak. Their message was so effective that a large number of Jews and Gentiles believed. They spent a considerable amount of time in that city, preaching Jesus and performing miraculous signs and wonders in his name (Acts 14:1–3).

But some of the Jews and Gentiles in that city eventually got fed up with what Paul and Barnabas were doing. Together they formed a plot "to mistreat and stone them" (v. 5). The two missionaries found out about what was being planned, so they immediately fled south to Lystra along the Via Sebaste, the great Roman road that led from Ephesus to the Euphrates River. They were still in the Roman province of Galatia, but in the Lycaonian region.

Lystra did not have a strong Jewish element, so Paul preached out in the open marketplace. There he saw a crippled man and by the power of Jesus raised him to his feet, just as Peter had done in Acts 3. When the residents of Lystra saw this, they excitedly felt that the gods had come down to visit them in human form. According to a local legend, Zeus and Hermes once visited their city in human form, and only one elderly couple offered them hospitality. In judgment, the two gods destroyed the houses of all the inhospitable people. Thus, the only proper response to this new visit from the gods was to offer sacrifices to them.

Paul and Barnabas did not at first know what was going on because the Lystrans were speaking in the Lycaonian language. But when the missionaries got wind of what was happening, they shouted for the Lystrans to stop. Paul took the opportunity to bring a message that emphasized his and Barnabas's humanity and God's universal love and care. Only with difficulty were they able to persuade the people to stop their sacrificing.

Then some Jews from Antioch and Iconium arrived in Lystra and managed to convince the crowd that Paul and Barnabas were dangerous men. Thus, they stoned Paul and dragged him outside the city, thinking he was dead. He recovered, however, and the next day left for Derbe.

In Derbe and the Return Trip

Derbe was on the eastern border of South Galatia, close to the Roman province of Cilicia (where Paul had grown up). In that city Paul and Barnabas once again found an opportunity to proclaim the gospel and won a large number of disciples. Whether they began in a synagogue is not mentioned in Acts 14:21.

After establishing a Christian community in Derbe, Paul and Barnabas decided not to push further east into Cilicia, probably because Paul had already adequately evangelized that area. (Note Acts 15:23, which indicates in a letter written a year later that there were a number of churches in Cilicia.) Instead, the two missionaries retraced their steps along the Via Sebaste and visited the churches that they had just started—in Lystra, Iconium, and Antioch of Pisidia.

In each of these cities, Paul and Barnabas gathered the believers together, strengthened them in the faith, encouraged them to remain true to the gospel, and appointed elders for the ongoing administration of church affairs. With prayer and fasting they commissioned these new leaders in their work for the Lord (Acts 14:21–23).

Paul and Barnabas then traveled south, back to Perga, a city they had passed through after arriving from Cyprus but had not preached in. This time they took the opportunity to preach there. After doing so, they went the short distance to the port city of Attalia, when they caught a ship headed for Syria (14:26).

The final destination of the two missionaries was the church that had sent them out, the church in Antioch. When they arrived there, they gathered the believers together and reported all the great things that God had done through them in Cyprus and Galatia. For the next year or so, they remained in Antioch and ministered to the church in that city (14:27–28).

The Jerusalem Council

The Problem of the Gentiles

In the history of the New Testament church up to this point, two things are plain: (1) Paul did not hesitate to preach the gospel to Gentiles and to baptize them into the name of Jesus when they believed; this pattern had been taking place with the full approval of the Lord (Acts 8:26–39; 9:15; 10:1–11:18); and (2) the Jews were most unhappy when a rabbi (as Paul was) was willing to accept fully as God's covenant people those who had never been circumcised. The anger over this issue became so intense at times on Paul's first missionary journey that he and Barnabas had to flee for their lives (13:42–51; 14:1–7, 19).

After that first missionary journey, however, a new facet linked with this issue emerged. There were some Jewish *Christians* who likewise did not support what was going on in the churches Paul had organized. These were called Judaizers (what we might today call the right-wing conservatives)—church members who were opposed to such a radical departure from what they had known all their lives and from the pattern their ancestors had followed for centuries. These people questioned whether it was really God's will that a person could become a Christian without first becoming a Jew through undergoing circumcision.

A fierce argument over this issue first surfaced in the church at Antioch of Syria, Paul's sending church. Many there, of course, supported Paul, especially after they heard what had been accomplished on his first missionary journey. But some men with the gift of teaching came from Judea to Antioch and insisted that Paul had it all wrong: "Unless you are circumcised, according to the custom taught by Moses, you cannot be saved" (Acts 15:1; cf. Gal. 2:4).

This was a much greater threat to the church than the complaint of the Hellenistic widows in Acts 6, for the church now faced the possibility that its unity might rupture and that two churches might develop—a Jewish Christian church and a Gentile Christian church. Something had to be done—and soon!

The Private Meeting

Apparently the debate with the Judean visitors to the church in Antioch could not be resolved in a congenial manner. Neither Paul nor the Judaizers would give in to the thinking of the other side (Acts 15:2; Gal. 2:5). Therefore the church leaders in Antioch, caught in the middle, felt that they needed the input of the apostles and elders in Jerusalem on this issue. They sent Paul and Barnabas as their delegates to the council that was to meet in Jerusalem. If anyone could argue the case for not circumcising Gentile believers, it would be those two.

As Paul and Barnabas set out on the three-hundred-mile trip from Antioch to Jerusalem, they traveled through Phoenicia and Samaria. The two missionaries took the time on the way to visit the churches in these areas and to share with them what had been happening among the Gentiles. The news made these churches glad.

Immediately after they arrived in Jerusalem, Paul and Barnabas sought a private meeting with the main leaders of the Christian church, who had also assembled there—the apostles Peter and John son of Zebedee, and James the Lord's brother, leader of the church in Jerusalem (Gal. 2:2, 8–9; cf. Acts 15:4). In this private meeting the five of them discussed the issue thoroughly and came to the conclusion that the Lord had indeed revealed to Paul the gospel he preached among the Gentiles. Peter, John, and James could live with that, even though they themselves felt more comfortable preaching to those who were circumcised (i.e., to Jews).

To cement his thinking on the issue, Paul had taken along Titus, an uncircumcised but devout Gentile Christian whom Paul probably converted somewhere on his first missionary journey (see Titus 1:4) and who had journeyed to Antioch. Paul asked the apostles directly whether Titus had to be circumcised. The "pillars" of the church agreed that Titus did not need to be circumcised (Gal. 2:1–3, 9). With this meeting behind him, Paul was ready to face the open meeting with the elders of the church in Jerusalem.

The Public Meeting

The open meeting began cordially enough. Paul and Barnabas were welcomed by the apostles and elders (Acts 15:4). But when the main business of the day got under way, the Judaizers (many of whom, like Paul, had been trained as Pharisees) said, "The Gentiles must be circumcised and required to obey the law of Moses" (15:5).

The main issue, the salvation of the Gentiles, was now out in the open. "Much discussion" ensued, with many people standing up to give their viewpoint on the topic (15:6–7a). The moderator for the assembly was probably James the Lord's brother. Finally, it was Peter's turn to address the assembly. He stood and reminded the people of what had happened to him about ten years before, when God had specifically told him to go to Cornelius, even though he was uncircumcised, and share with him the gospel. And then God had filled those uncircumcised but believing Gentiles with his Holy Spirit. "He made no distinction between us and them, for he purified their hearts by faith" (15:9). Peter went on, therefore, to side clearly with Paul: Salvation is by grace, and by grace alone, not by any keeping of the law (15:10–11).

Since it was story time, Paul and Barnabas stood up and recounted for the apostles and elders what had happened on the missionary journey they had recently completed. They told about all the signs and wonders God had performed through them and undoubtedly affirmed, through numerous examples, that God had indeed given his grace and Holy Spirit to uncircumcised Gentiles. Who can dispute living examples of God's activity?

Finally, James spoke up. Undoubtedly many in the gathering were wondering precisely where he stood on this issue. He, after all, had a strong personal emphasis on law-abiding Christianity, as his letter (the New Testament book of James) clearly testifies. But on the matter of salvation, James sided with Peter and Paul, quoting Amos 9:11–12, a prophecy in which God talked about a coming time when the Gentiles would seek the Lord and be saved. "Therefore," he said, "we should not make it difficult for the Gentiles who are turning to God" (Acts 15:19). But, partly in deference to those on the other side of the issue, James did propose that a letter be sent to the churches.

The Decision and the Letter

One of the main problems affecting a church that had both Jewish Christians and Gentile Christians was the matter of fellowshiping together as one body, particularly eating together. (Having a meal together meant far more sociologically in Bible times than it does today in our fast-food culture.) The Jews adhered to a host of Old Testament regulations regarding what they could and could not eat. Since Jewish Christians still considered themselves Jews, and since keeping the food laws had been such a large part of their tradition, they felt obligated to continue to follow these laws (cf. Peter's comments in Acts 10:11–16).

The Council of Jerusalem felt led by the Holy Spirit (cf. 15:28) to do something to maintain fellowship among believers. Therefore, even though the basic question about whether keeping the law was necessary *for salvation* had been decided, the apostles and elders also insisted that Gentile Christians should respect the food laws of the Jews. They were instructed not to eat meat that had been sacrificed to idols, not to eat meat that had been improperly drained of blood, and not to eat or drink blood itself; and they were to abstain from sexual immorality (a sin prevalent especially in pagan religious festivals) (Acts 15:20–21; cf. vv. 28–29).

Such rules were required to preserve fellowship in the church. They were written up in a letter addressed to Gentile believers in Antioch, Syria, and Cilicia. The council was not satisfied with a mere letter, however; it also chose two respected, trusted men—Judas Barsabbas and Silas—to carry the letter personally to Antioch and to answer any question that might arise in the churches on its implementation.

Paul, Barnabas, Judas, and Silas then headed for Antioch. They assembled the church and read the letter, for which the Gentile Christians praised God. Judas and Silas stayed on for a while, encouraging and strengthening the believers there (15:32–33). It seems as if one of the items they clarified was that if Jews and Gentiles ate together and no one among them had any scruples, they could eat whatever food they wanted (cf. Gal. 2:12). Judas and Silas then returned to Jerusalem.

Paul—The Second Missionary Journey

Paul's Separation From Barnabas

After the letter had been delivered and Judas and Silas had returned to Jerusalem, Paul and Barnabas remained in Antioch, evangelizing those who did not know the Lord and preaching to and teaching the believers.

No one knows for sure all the details, but it was perhaps during this time that an unfortunate confrontation took place between Peter and Paul, and then another between Paul and Barnabas (Gal. 2:11–14). Peter, as we have seen, had gradually come to accept the fact that he could eat with Gentiles, regardless of what they ate, and not be defiled in the eyes of God. Perhaps on his way to northern Asia Minor, where he had been evangelizing, he stopped for a visit in Antioch. There he did indeed eat freely with Gentile Christians (2:12).

But then a group of the more conservative Jewish Christians came from Jerusalem. Perhaps they offered a new interpretation of the letter of the Council, that keeping the food laws was required of Gentiles regardless of whether Jewish Christians were around or not. For some reason, Peter was afraid of these visitors and decided it would be best for him, in the interest of peace, to stop associating with the Gentile Christians. This disturbed Paul immensely, and he publicly confronted Peter: "You are a Jew, yet you live like a Gentile and not like a Jew. How is it, then, that you force Gentiles to follow Jewish customs?" (Gal. 2:14). Paul would have none of Peter's duplicity.

In whatever happened between Peter and Paul, the other Jewish Christians, including even Barnabas, sided with Peter and the "men . . . from James." The dispute between Paul and Barnabas then spilled over into another area. When Paul proposed leaving Antioch and visiting the churches formed on their previous missionary trip, Barnabas wanted to take Mark along again (Acts 15:36–38). Paul, however, felt this would be a hindrance to him, for Mark had been a "quitter" (cf. 13:13). The upshot of this conflict was that Barnabas decided to take Mark with him and visit the churches they had established on the island of Cyprus, while Paul chose Silas and set out for the churches they had organized in Asia Minor.

The Start of Paul's Second Missionary Journey

The choice of Silas as Paul's partner was a good one. He obviously had the respect and endorsement of the church in Jerusalem (Acts 15:22, 25–27). Like Paul, he was also a Roman citizen (cf. 16:37–38). Moreover, though this was probably not a motivating factor at the time, Silas knew how to read and write and could serve as an amanuensis (secretary) for Paul when he wrote letters to his churches (cf. 1 Thess. 1:1; 2 Thess. 1:1; 1 Peter 5:12).

The first thing Paul and Silas did as they began their journey was to visit other Christian communities in Syria and Cilicia. As they traveled they read the letter from the Jerusalem Council that had been addressed to them (cf. Acts 15:23). Many of these churches were presumably ones that Paul had started during his "silent years." Then the two of them crossed over the provincial border between Cilicia and Galatia and arrived at Derbe and then Lystra (16:1; cf. 14:8–20).

At Lystra, Paul and Silas added a third member to their party—a young man named Timothy. Timothy had become a believer in Jesus during Paul's brief stay in Lystra on his first missionary journey (see 1 Cor. 4:17; 1 Tim. 1:2). His mother, Eunice, was a Jewish woman (2 Tim. 1:5), but his father was a pagan and had never permitted Timothy to be circumcised (Acts 16:3). Timothy himself had a good reputation with the churches in Lystra and Iconium, and thus Paul invited the young believer to join him and Silas.

Since Paul intended as much as possible to begin each new ministry in a synagogue, and since the Jews in any synagogue would be horrified if they knew an uncircumcised Jewish young man was in their building, Paul felt it would be wise to circumcise Timothy. The threesome then began traveling along the Via Sebaste, continuing to visit the churches in Galatia and presumably talking to the Christians about the decision that had been made in Jerusalem regarding circumcision. Paul emphasized the message that it was not necessary for someone to be circumcised in order to be saved; Silas would have added the information that was contained in the letter that came from the council.

The Vision of a Man From Macedonia

In their trip along the Via Sebaste, Paul, Silas, and Timothy reached Antioch of Pisidia, where Paul and Barnabas had started their ministry in Asia Minor several years earlier. Rather than turn south at Antioch, however, they decided to continue traveling east, heading toward Ephesus, the major metropolis of Asia Minor. But for some unknown reason, the Holy Spirit told them not to preach the Word of God in that area (Acts 16:6).

Thus they headed north, thinking that perhaps they might preach the good news in Mysia and Bithynia. But again the Spirit of Jesus would not allow them to do that (16:7). In a quandary as to what the Lord wanted them to do, they kept heading north until they arrived in Troas, a city on the coast of the Aegean Sea, near the Dardanelles.

One night Paul received a vision in which he saw a man from Macedonia standing and begging him, "Come over to Macedonia and help us" (16:9). Macedonia was on the other side of the Aegean Sea, the province just north of Greece (which is called Achaia in the New Testament). As Paul, Silas, and Timothy discussed the vision, they all agreed that it had come from the Lord and that he wanted them to go farther west.

They found a ship that was heading that way and sailed to Neapolis, a port city on the coast of Macedonia. Paul and company decided to head for Philippi, the major city in that area. Their intent was to establish a strong Christian community in that city, so that from that church the message of salvation could branch out into the smaller towns and villages of Macedonia.

Another person accompanied Paul, Silas, and Timothy on their journey—Luke, a doctor (cf. Col. 4:14) who had had a practice in Troas (note the "we" in Acts 16:10). He presumably stayed behind in Philippi when the other three left for other cities (note the absence of "we" in 17:1). He undoubtedly helped the church in Philippi and perhaps also set up a medical practice in the city.

Experiences in Philippi

One of the surprising things about Philippi was that, despite its size and importance, it did not have a strong enough Jewish presence to have a synagogue. (It took a minimum of ten Jewish men to form an official synagogue.) Thus Paul inquired as to where he might find at least some Jews, and he was told that a group of Jewish women met regularly on the Sabbath for prayer outside the city gate and along the river.

One of the people they met there was a wealthy businesswoman named Lydia. She was from Thyatira in Asia Minor and dealt in purple-dyed cloth. She believed the message that Paul spoke to them on that Sabbath and requested baptism. She then insisted that Paul's company should stay with her in her home, and she probably also opened her house as a place where others could come to hear the message of the gospel (Acts 16:14–15).

As Paul was going to the place of prayer one day, he was followed by a slave girl who was filled with an evil spirit. Her owners were using her to predict the future. For days on end she pestered Paul by following him and crying out, "These men are servants of the Most High God, who are telling you the way to be saved" (16:17). Finally, Paul turned around, rebuked the spirit, and told it to come out of her. The spirit had no choice but to obey.

The owners of this girl, however, saw their means of income disappear. They grabbed Paul and Silas, dragged them before the city magistrates, and charged the two of them, as Jews, with advocating illegal religious customs. Anti-Semitic feelings surfaced, and the magistrates, to quell a riot, ordered Paul and Silas to be stripped and flogged. They then threw them into the securest part of the city jail, with strict orders to the jailer to guard them carefully (16:22–24).

Around midnight, Paul and Silas, certainly in pain, began singing songs. Suddenly an earthquake opened the doors of the prison, and everyone had the opportunity to escape. Somehow Paul managed to persuade all the prisoners to stay put. When the jailer called for lights and saw the door open but all the prisoners still in their cells, he knew there was something different about Paul and Silas and asked them the question, "What must I do to be saved?" (16:30). Paul told him about Jesus, and by the end of the night, the jailer and his household had been baptized into Jesus Christ.

On to Thessalonica

The following morning, the city magistrates of Philippi ordered Paul and Silas to be released. Tempers had cooled down, and presumably they realized they had no valid charges against the apostles. But what they did not know was that Paul and Silas were Roman citizens, and no Roman citizen could be flogged without due process of law.

When the magistrates heard this, they became frightened, hoping that news of what they had done would never reach the emperor. They personally went to the jail, apologized to Paul and Silas, and begged them to leave the city. Paul, Silas, and Timothy obliged and headed further south until they came to Thessalonica, on the coast of the Aegean Sea and still in Macedonia.

Thessalonica did have a Jewish synagogue, so the three missionaries went there on the Sabbath. As usual, Paul was invited to speak as a visiting rabbi, and on at least three Sabbaths he told them about Jesus, reasoning from the Scriptures that he was the promised Messiah (Acts 17:1–3). His preaching was successful, for a few Jews and a large number of God-fearing Gentiles (including many prominent women) believed.

Paul probably stayed in Thessalonica for several months, most likely using the house of a believer named Jason as the meeting place (17:7). During his stay, Paul did not have to work, since he received several monetary gifts from the church he had started in Philippi to help pay his living expenses (Phil. 4:15–17).

But the Jews who had not become believers through Paul's preaching, when they saw the popularity of the Christian movement, "rounded up some bad characters from the marketplace, formed a mob and started a riot in the city" (17:5). When the rioters could not find Paul and Silas in Jason's house, they dragged Jason and some other believers before the city magistrates and charged them with sedition against Rome. They were unable to prove their charges, but the city magistrates made Jason promise that Paul and Silas would leave the town and never come back; he had to post a bond to certify that promise (cf. Acts 17:8–9; 1 Thess. 2:17–18). That very night Paul and Silas left Thessalonica and went to Berea, a city in Macedonia further to the west.

Berea and on to Achaia

As was their custom, upon arriving in Berea, Paul and Silas headed for the synagogue. The Jews there were more open-minded than those in Thessalonica. They were willing to listen to Paul as he preached and willing to examine the Scriptures to see if what he was preaching was really true (Acts 17:10–11). As a result, many Jews and many Gentiles (both men and women) became believers.

Somehow word arrived in Thessalonica that Paul and his company were preaching and gaining converts in Berea. The Jews of Thessalonica, therefore, sent a delegation of right-wing Jews to Berea to stir up trouble. Rather than wait until things got out of hand again as they had in Thessalonica, Paul left Berea immediately. But he departed alone, leaving Silas and Timothy behind; they were to join him in Achaia as soon as possible.

Paul then traveled to Athens, the cultural center of Greece. He made a self-guided tour of the city and was appalled at the vast amount of idolatry evident there. Therefore he took it upon himself to discuss his religious beliefs with the pagan Athenians who gathered daily in the marketplace. Discussing religion is apparently how many of them spent their time. Paul also visited the synagogue in Athens, where he reasoned with Jews and God-fearing Gentiles (Acts 17:16–17).

After Paul had been in Athens for a while, Timothy and Silas joined up with him. They brought word about the church in Berea, but also about how the Christians in Thessalonica were faring. These believers were already beginning to suffer some form of persecution for their faith. Paul longed to be able to go back and see them and to teach them more about the gospel, but the bond Jason had posted hindered both him and Silas from returning.

Therefore Paul sent Timothy back to Thessalonica, in order to assure the Christians there of his concern, to teach them more about Christ, and to encourage them in the Christian life. Paul was afraid that perhaps they might decide that following Christ wasn't such a good idea after all (1 Thess. 3:1–6).

This was the first time that Timothy was alone on a mission—only a few short months after he had joined Paul and Silas! Shortly thereafter, Paul sent Silas off to Macedonia, perhaps to visit Philippi and Berea (Acts 18:5). Paul was now alone again in Athens.

The Speech Before the Areopagus

The two main philosophical schools in Athens that seemed interested in Paul's message were the Stoics and Epicureans. Both groups were having a hard time getting a good grasp of what religion or philosophy Paul was proclaiming. They concluded he was telling them about two new gods: Jesus and Anastasis (*anastasis* is the Greek word for "resurrection"; see Acts 17:17–18). Since it was part of the job of the city officials to investigate any new religions that floated into town, they summoned Paul to address the Areopagus (the town council; see 17:19–21, 33).

Paul's message to these pagans is different from any other that Luke records in Acts. Paul began by referring to his tour of Athens and his discovery of an altar "TO AN UNKNOWN GOD." He used this as a touch-off point to tell them about this God, the God of all creation, who was not a visible idol but an invisible spiritual being. Paul even quoted some of their own poets to help them understand that this God is not a distant being, but someone who is close to us.

Paul went on, then, to talk both about the need for repentance and about the reality of divine future judgment through Jesus. Finally he told them that proof of the coming judgment is the fact that God raised his Son Jesus from the dead.

At that point, Paul lost his audience; in fact, many of them began to laugh in derision. Greek philosophy in general taught that the soul is imprisoned in the body and that death is a good thing, because then the soul can escape that prison. So why would any freed soul ever want to return to a human body (i.e., the resurrected body of Jesus)? It just did not make sense philosophically.

There were a few people, however, who did become believers. One of them was even a member of the Areopagus—Dionysius by name. It is entirely possible that among Paul's converts were a few Jews from the synagogue. But for the most part, his influence in Athens was nil. He decided to leave and move on to another city to the southwest, Corinth.

In Corinth

When Paul left Athens, he was alone and discouraged. His next stop was the city of Corinth, the capital of Achaia, where he arrived "in weakness and fear" (1 Cor. 2:3). He decided that in this city his message would be nothing more than "Jesus Christ and him crucified" (2:2).

Corinth was on the small isthmus that connected the central portion of Greece with the Peloponnesus. It was a thriving city, since about a mile both east and west were the port cities of Cenchrea and Lechaeum. Corinth was also known for its immorality and its worship of Aphrodite, a goddess whose temple at one time boasted having a thousand sacred prostitutes.

Paul linked up in Corinth with a Jewish couple, Aquila and Priscilla, who (like Paul) were leather workers (the Greek word used here is more generic than "tentmaker," as in NIV) and who had recently been expelled from Rome along with all other Jews. The Roman historian Suetonius attributes this expulsion to the emperor Claudius, who gave the order during his ninth year (A.D. 49) because the Jews had been rioting "at the instigation of Chrestus." (Does this mean "Christ"?—many scholars consider this a reference to intense conflict between strict Jews and Jewish Christians.) Most likely, Aquila and Priscilla were already believers when Paul met them. The apostle stayed at their house and worked with them in their trade (Acts 18:1–3).

As was his custom, Paul entered the synagogue on the Sabbath and, having been invited to preach, told the "Jews and Greeks" assembled there that Jesus was the Messiah. As usual, after a short period of time, he was barred from further preaching there. He therefore told the Jews that he would spend his time preaching to Gentiles. One of his converts, perhaps surprisingly, was Crispus, the synagogue leader. Next door to the synagogue lived Titius Justus, a worshiper of God who became a believer; he invited any who wanted to hear Paul to come to his house (18:7–8).

Things were going well in Corinth, but in the back of Paul's mind was always the possibility of persecution, and he was mentally preparing himself to have to leave. But one night the Lord spoke to him in a dream and assured him that his experiences in Macedonia were not going to be repeated in Achaia. God had many people in that city whom Paul was to reach. Paul's total stay in Corinth was a year and a half—the longest he had been in one city up to that time (18:9–11).

Letters to Macedonia and Galatia

While Paul was in Corinth, both Timothy and Silas returned from their visits to Philippi and Thessalonica (and probably Berea). They brought with them another gift from the church in Philippi (cf. Phil. 4:16–17)—large enough so that Paul was able to devote 100 percent of his time to preaching and evangelism (Acts 18:5).

Timothy reported how well the church in Thessalonica was doing (1 Thess. 3:6–10). They had become such model believers, in spite of persecution, that people everywhere were talking about the strength of their faith. In fact, Paul had heard about their boldness for the Lord not only from Timothy but also from a number of other people who had been in Macedonia (1:6–10).

But there were problems in Thessalonica. Some of his opponents were trying to discredit Paul, charging him with preaching for profit and running away at the slightest hint of trouble. Paul reminded the Thessalonians how he had worked for his living expenses and how intensely he cared about them (1 Thess. 2). The Thessalonian believers had theological questions as well. Some among them had died, and they wondered if these Christians had therefore lost their chance of going to be with Jesus when he returned to earth. Paul answered these questions by teaching the doctrine of the resurrection (4:13–5:10).

The letter was brought to Thessalonica, perhaps by Timothy. He reported back to Paul that new problems had developed. Eschatological fervor for the return of Jesus was reaching an all-time high, and some people had even quit work to wait for the event (2 Thess. 3:6–12). Moreover, some were claiming that the Day of the Lord had already come (2:1–2). The apostle addressed both these issues in his second letter to that church.

Also while Paul was in Corinth, someone brought him word that many in the churches of Galatia were being influenced by the Judaizers, becoming convinced that true Christians had to undergo circumcision and obey the other Old Testament laws (Gal. 1:6–7; 3:1–5). Paul therefore wrote to them a very impassioned letter (the letter to Galatians), in which he emphasized that salvation is by grace alone through faith and that believers have freedom from the law in Christ.

The Gallio Episode

About halfway through Paul's year and one-half in Corinth, a most significant event occurred. The Jews made a concerted effort to drag Paul in front of the recently appointed Roman proconsul, Gallio, claiming that the apostle was advocating an illegal religion. In order to stop the flow of new religions that was undermining traditional Roman religion in the first century, the emperor had declared all new religions illegal and subject to persecution. Older religions such as Judaism, however, were exempt from this ruling and were declared legal.

Gallio listened to the charges brought by the Jews against Paul, that he was advocating a new religion. Paul, of course, insisted that he, like the Jews, believed the Old Testament, but simply had different views on its interpretation. Gallio came to the conclusion that this matter was an intra-Jewish squabble and threw the issue out of court (Acts 18:12–16).

This event was significant for two reasons. First, Gallio was a prominent Roman figure. His brother was Seneca, the famous Roman orator, though Gallio was later adopted by another famous orator, Lucius Junius Gallio. He was known for his personal charisma. When someone of his stature declared that Christianity was a legal religion in the Roman Empire, that ruling would undoubtedly set a legal precedent for Roman officials in other provinces. For the next ten years at least (until the time of Nero), Christianity enjoyed full legal protection.

Gallio's action is also critical for Pauline chronology. According to Roman records, Gallio was proconsul of Achaia for only one year (July 51 to July 52). Most scholars date Paul's missionary journeys both backward and forward from this date. If this episode happened toward the beginning of Gallio's tenure as proconsul and in the middle of Paul's stay in Corinth (cf. Acts 18:18), then Paul arrived in Corinth in the fall of A.D. 50 and left in the spring of A.D. 52. This dating also corresponds, of course, with the date for the arrival of Aquila and Priscilla in Corinth (see the section "In Corinth").

The End of the Second Missionary Journey

In the spring of A.D. 52, Paul decided to leave Corinth and return to his home church, Antioch. Accompanied by Aquila and Priscilla, he went to Cenchrea, Corinth's port city to the east, and caught a ship headed for Asia Minor. Aquila and Priscilla were planning to go to Ephesus, where they perhaps had business interests. Paul spent a short time in that city and preached in the synagogue. But he was determined to go to Antioch, so he promised to come back at a later time, if that was God's will for him (Acts 18:19–21). (Remember that the Holy Spirit had earlier forbidden Paul from preaching in Asia Minor—16:6.)

Paul then caught a ship sailing from Ephesus to Caesarea, the port city closest to Jerusalem. Acts 18:22 reads: "When he landed at Caesarea, he went up and greeted the church and then went down to Antioch." This "going up" and "going down" almost certainly refers to a quick visit Paul made to the church in Jerusalem. Undoubtedly, as he had done after his first missionary journey, he reported on the success of his recent trip.

Although Luke does not talk about this in Acts, it also seems apparent that Paul discovered that the concern over the relationship of Christians to the Jewish law had not been resolved once and for all through the Council in Jerusalem. In fact, a "conservative backlash" was occurring, as Paul had already discovered through the reports he heard about the churches in Galatia. Jerusalem seems to have been the seedbed of this movement, and it concerned Paul deeply.

Paul wanted to do something to convince the believers in Judea that the Gentile believers would feel they were one with the Jewish Christians. He remembered that some years earlier, the gift from Antioch to Jerusalem during the time of famine had been much appreciated (Acts 11:27–30). It was, therefore, probably during this time that Paul decided to take a collection among his Gentile churches the next time he visited them and to bring it to Jerusalem for the benefit of the poor among the saints there. In that way he hoped to foster a greater spirit of unity (cf. Rom. 15:25–27). With this in mind, Paul left Jerusalem for the three-hundred-mile trip to Antioch (Acts 18:22b).

Paul—The Third Missionary Journey

The Trip to Ephesus

After spending upwards of a year in Antioch, Paul decided to head back to Asia and Europe. (This was probably the spring of A.D. 53, seeing that the mountains were all but impassable during the winter months.) From Antioch he headed west, going first through Cilicia (perhaps spending some time in Tarsus, his hometown), then on to Galatia (Acts 18:23, likely including the region of Pisidia). In the major cities through which he traveled were churches he had started.

One wonders, of course, what sort of reception he received in the Galatian churches, seeing that he had written his stinging letter to them only a year and a half earlier (even calling them "you foolish Galatians," Gal. 3:1). But Paul was never one to shrink from controversy, especially when the truth of the gospel was at stake (cf. 1:6–9; 5:12).

Regardless of his reception, one main burden on his mind was doing whatever was necessary to heal the rift that seemed to be growing in the church. He therefore ordered (NIV "told") the Christians in Galatia to take up weekly offerings for the poor among the saints in Jerusalem (1 Cor. 16:1–2). The seed for taking up this collection in Galatia had already been planted, for in the letter Paul had written to the believers there he acknowledged that the "pillars" of the church (Peter, John, and James) had suggested, during their private meeting prior to the official Council of Jerusalem, that they "should continue to remember the poor" (Gal. 2:10). What happened to the money they collected and when and how (or even if) it was brought to Jerusalem we do not know.

Paul then continued west through Phrygia (Acts 18:23). The road led through such cities as Colosse and Laodicea. Apparently he did not stop in any of these cities, except perhaps for an overnight stay (cf. Col. 2:1). He was heading for the major city in Asia, Ephesus, where he had spent a few days with Aquila and Priscilla after leaving Corinth. In this city he intended to set up shop for a while, working on his leather business and preaching the gospel.

In the Meantime

A couple of important developments had taken place during the year of Paul's absence from Ephesus. First, while Aquila and Priscilla were conducting their business in Ephesus, they attended the synagogue regularly. One day a visiting Jewish scholar from Alexandria, Egypt, named Apollos, spoke at the synagogue (Acts 18:24, 26); like Paul he tried to convince people that Jesus was the Messiah. But somehow Apollos had not been aware of the outpouring of the Holy Spirit on Pentecost, for he knew only the baptism of John the Baptist, not the Spirit-empowering baptism of Jesus (18:25).

Aquila and Priscilla therefore invited Apollos to their home, whereupon they told him many of the things that Paul had taught them in Corinth about Jesus and the Holy Spirit (18:26b). Apollos was a good learner, eagerly trying to find out all he could about Jesus the Messiah.

Second, trouble was beginning to develop in Corinth. After Paul and his company left, other teachers settled in that city who took issue with the teaching Paul had been giving. Perhaps they were Judaizers, seeing that a certain segment in the church in Corinth eventually aligned themselves with what they considered to be the teachings of Peter (1 Cor. 1:12).

Word must have come to Aquila and Priscilla in Ephesus about this development in Corinth, so they encouraged Apollos to go there and see what he could do to help bring the faith of the Corinthians back in line with what Paul preached. They wrote a letter of introduction to those in charge in Corinth, encouraging them to accept Apollos as a bona fide preacher of the gospel (Acts 18:27).

Part of Apollos's goal in Corinth was to reach new people for Christ, and he gave a powerful witness to Jews that Jesus was indeed the Christ (18:28). He was also a great help to those who were already believers, though (to be sure) he undoubtedly gave an Alexandrian emphasis to his interpretation of Scripture. The end result, however, despite the best of his intentions, was the development of another faction in Corinth—an "Apollos party" (1 Cor. 1:12).

Paul's First Days in Ephesus

One of the first things that happened upon Paul's arrival in Ephesus was his meeting twelve men whom he assumed were disciples of the Lord Jesus. Presumably they spoke about the Messiah, but in Paul's discussions with them he came to realize that they had not received the Holy Spirit when they believed (Acts 19:1–2). This puzzled Paul, so he asked them whether or not they had been baptized. They affirmed they had been, but only into the baptism of John the Baptist, whose baptism symbolized exclusively the repentance of sins (cf. Apollos in 18:24–25).

The apostle therefore corrected their theology, telling them that John's baptism was only provisional and that the Baptist himself always pointed people to Jesus as someone greater than he, God's promised Messiah (cf. John 1:24–34; 3:22–36). Moreover, baptism in the name of Jesus as Lord was linked with the reception of the Holy Spirit (cf. Acts 2:37–39). When these men heard this teaching, they asked to be baptized into the name of Jesus; when they were, the Holy Spirit came on them, and they spoke in tongues and began to prophesy (Acts 19:4–6).

On the Sabbath Paul, as was his custom, entered the synagogue in Ephesus. In contrast to some of the cities of Macedonia, he was able to preach there for three whole months, demonstrating from the Scriptures that "the kingdom of God" had come in Jesus (Acts 19:8; cf. Mark 1:14–15). Many people came to believe in Jesus as the Messiah.

But preaching in the synagogue could not go on indefinitely. The staunch Jews in the synagogue eventually had enough; they refused to believe Paul's message and began reporting nasty things about the Christian movement (Acts 19:9). So Paul made a decision to leave the synagogue and rent the lecture hall of a man named Tyrannus, presumably during those times of the day when it was not in use. People came not only from Ephesus but from all over the province of Asia to hear Paul preach and teach about Jesus, and many of them became believers.

Ministry in Ephesus and Asia

Paul ministered in Ephesus for at least two years and three months (Acts 19:8, 10). Churches sprang up all throughout the province of Asia from Christians who listened to Paul preach and then returned to their own cities. From Paul's writings, for example, we know that churches were organized in both Laodicea and Colosse—churches that Paul never even had a chance to visit (see Col. 2:1). Perhaps also at this time churches developed in Smyrna, Pergamum, Thyatira (where Lydia was from; cf. Acts 16:14), Sardis, and Philadelphia. (These churches, together with Ephesus and Laodicea, formed the seven churches of Asia to which John wrote [Rev. 2–3].)

Paul's ministry was more than just preaching, however. He also performed many healing miracles and exorcisms. In some cases, people brought napkins or aprons for him to touch, which were then brought back to the sick in order to heal them.

As is apparent from Bar-Jesus on the island of Cyprus (and as is confirmed by archaeology; cf. *Zondervan Quick-Reference Library: Biblical Archaeology*), Jews were known throughout the ancient world for their occult powers. In Ephesus was a man named Sceva, who with seven sons went around casting out evil spirits in the name of various spiritual beings. When they saw how Paul was able to cast out demons in the name of Jesus Christ, they added Jesus to their list of spells. But when they tried to cast out one particularly obstinate evil spirit "in the name of Jesus, whom Paul preaches" (Acts 19:13), the evil spirit replied, "Jesus I know, and I know about Paul, but who are you?" The demon-possessed man then single-handedly overpowered the seven sons of Sceva, and "they ran out of the house, naked and bleeding" (19:15–16).

That incident created quite a stir throughout Ephesus, and people recognized the great power of the name of Jesus. Many believers who had secretly been involved in the occult brought their magic books to a huge, public book-burning ceremony. The value of those books would have been enough to pay the average annual wages of about 150 people (Acts 19:17–20).

Immorality in Corinth

The city of Corinth was situated directly across the Aegean Sea from Ephesus. While Paul was working in Ephesus, he frequently had visitors from the church in that city, informing him of what was going on in their midst.

The reports, for the most part, were not good. One of the first things Paul heard about was a problem they were having with maintaining appropriate Christian standards of sexual morality. Perhaps this was understandable, since the city of Corinth, situated between two seaports, was known for its loose sexual morals (see the section "In Corinth"). In fact, the Greek language has a verb, *korinthiazomai*, which means to live like a Corinthian in an immoral lifestyle.

Paul, therefore, felt it necessary to write a letter to the Christians in Corinth (a letter we no longer have), in which he warned them "not to associate with sexually immoral people" (1 Cor. 5:9). For some reason, many in the church reacted negatively to this letter: "How can we do business in this city," they apparently asked, "if we have to avoid all contact with people whose morals standards are not what Paul thinks they should be?" (cf. 5:10).

When Paul heard that reaction, he corrected himself in his second letter to the Corinthians (our 1 Corinthians), in which he clarified himself: They were not to associate with any *fellow believer* who was living a sexually immoral life—not even eat with such a person (undoubtedly including eating at the Lord's table in holy communion; see 1 Cor. 5:11).

By the time Paul wrote this second letter, immorality in the church had gotten worse, for he had received word that one of their members was living in an incestuous relationship with his stepmother—a situation that shocked even the pagans (1 Cor. 5:1). What was particularly horrifying in Paul's mind was that the rest of the members of the church felt proud about their tolerance of this situation (5:2). Paul instructed the Corinthians to expel this wicked man from their midst and to stop their boasting, which was working like a cancer among them (5:3–7, 12–13). Moreover, Paul felt a need to warn and instruct the entire church not to get involved in prostitution, but to maintain pure lives (6:9–20).

Other Problems in Corinth

The situation of sexual immorality was not the only problem Paul faced with the Corinthians. Some people from Chloe's household arrived with the sad news that the church in Corinth was hopelessly divided into various warring factions; some claimed to be followers of Paul, some of Apollos, some of Peter, and some simply of Christ (1 Cor. 1:10–12). And in terms of personal relationships, some believers were filing lawsuits against others. Paul addressed these issues in 1 Corinthians 1:10–4:13; 6:1–8. Moreover, in order to monitor their progress, he told them he was sending Timothy as his personal representative (4:14–17) and promised to come soon himself and deal severely with any troublemakers (4:18–21).

The people from Chloe's household also brought along an official letter from the believers in Corinth, in which the church leaders asked Paul's advice on several issues: about sexual relations and marriage (1 Cor. 7:1), about virginity (7:25), about eating meat sacrificed to idols and Christian freedom (8:1), and about spiritual gifts, especially speaking in tongues and prophecy (12:1). The apostle also felt it necessary to write on a few other issues he had heard about that deeply concerned him—on the wearing of veils and relationships between men and women in the church (11:2–16), on impropriety in the way the Corinthians were conducting themselves at the Lord's table and in the common meal that preceded it (11:17–34), and on the resurrection (15:1–58; some in the church were insisting that the resurrection had already taken place).

Before Paul sent off the letter, he received another set of visitors (Stephanus, Fortunatus, and Achaicus), who seemed to indicate that things in Corinth were not all bleak (1 Cor. 16:17). That helped to refresh Paul's spirit. He also instructed the Corinthians to participate in the collection he was taking for the saints in Jerusalem (16:1–4) and reviewed for them his plans to come and visit them within the next six months (16:5–9).

More Trouble in Corinth

Sometime after the writing of 1 Corinthians, the situation in Corinth took a sudden, dramatic turn for the worse. Some new people arrived in the city who were even stronger in their opposition to Paul than were the "parties" that precipitated his extended discussion of the divisions in 1 Corinthians 1–4. These people (who must have claimed apostolic authority, since Paul calls them "super-apostles" and "false apostles," 2 Cor. 11:5, 13) did not merely attack Paul's ideas; they attacked Paul himself: "His letters are weighty and forceful, but in person he is unimpressive and his speaking amounts to nothing" (10:10).

Paul, therefore, changed his travel plans. Instead of going to Macedonia first (cf. 1 Cor. 16:5–6), he made a hasty trip directly across the Aegean Sea to Corinth, fully determined to bring the situation under control. But he failed, for he calls that visit to the Corinthian church a "painful visit" (2 Cor. 2:1; cf. 12:14; 13:1, which speak of a proposed third visit). So Paul quickly returned to Ephesus, a disappointed and angry man. In response, he fired off to them a letter that he "wrote . . . out of great distress and anguish of heart and with many tears" (2:4), and which "hurt" them (7:8; cf. v 12).

It seems likely that much, if not all, of this letter has been preserved as 2 Corinthians 10:1–13:10. In this letter Paul strongly asserted his authority as an apostle (even calling himself a "fool" for writing as he did; cf. 11:16–19), and he openly expressed his fury at being challenged. He pulled out all the stops against his opponents, comparing them to Satan, who "masquerades as an angel of light" (11:14).

But not even a letter was enough. Paul also needed a personal representative to contend for his case in Corinth. Timothy did not seem to have had much success on his earlier mission; perhaps he was too timid (cf. 1 Tim. 4:12; 2 Tim. 1:7). Thus, Paul chose Titus, who seems to have been much more of a diplomat and a statesman in dealing with conflict. Titus probably took along the "severe letter" as he left Ephesus for Corinth. He was also given instructions to do what he could to keep his collection for the saints in Jerusalem moving (cf. 2 Cor. 8:6).

Trouble in Ephesus

Paul continued to minister in Ephesus as Titus left for Corinth. Although Luke does not talk about it in Acts, strong opposition developed against Paul in that city—more likely from the civil authorities than from the Jews. We know from Acts 19:23–41 that the lucrative religious shrine business was suffering in Ephesus because of the spread of Christianity. Demetrius and his silversmith guild therefore started a riot, perhaps even intending to lynch Paul. That may be why the Asiarchs (the Roman officials in charge of Ephesus) suggested to Paul not to go into the amphitheater, where a mass of devotees to Artemis were shouting for two hours straight, "Great is Artemis of the Ephesians" (19:28–34). The city clerk managed finally to disperse the crowd (19:35–41).

Sometime later, however, hardships became so severe for Paul again that he "despaired even of life"; he "felt the sentence of death" (2 Cor. 1:8–9). It may be that Paul was imprisoned for some time in Ephesus, during which time he suffered much (1:4–7). If perchance this suffering occurred also earlier during his stay in Ephesus, Paul may even have had to "[fight] wild beasts" there (1 Cor. 15:32).

There seems to have been one bright spot during this time, however. Paul received a visit from Epaphroditus, a personal representative of the church in Philippi (Phil. 2:25–30). This man brought a gift from the Philippian church for Paul (4:10–18), and he even endangered his own life to minister to the apostle (2:30). As Paul suggests in Philippians (cf. 2 Cor. 1), he himself personally faced death as he never had before (cf. Phil. 1:20–24).

Perhaps this same letter of Philippians gives us further insight concerning Paul's opponents in Corinth. They preached Christ "out of envy and rivalry," thinking they could make things even more difficult for the imprisoned apostle (Phil. 1:15–17). And they also were vehement in their support for circumcision as a requirement for believers in Jesus (3:2–4).

This period had to have been a low time in the life of the apostle. After the riot in Ephesus and after his release from prison there, Paul decided it was time for him to leave Asia and head for Macedonia.

Meeting Titus in Macedonia

After Paul had left Corinth after his painful visit, he had made a promise to visit the Christians there again shortly (2 Cor. 1:15–16) before heading to Macedonia. But two things intervened to force him to change his mind. One was his imprisonment in Ephesus and severe danger he experienced there; the other was a lack of awareness about how his stern letter had been received and his realization that perhaps he might not yet be welcome in Corinth. (Titus had not yet reported back to him.) Therefore, Paul changed his travel plans and decided to head north, arriving in Troas.

The previous time Paul was in Troas, he had received the vision of the man from Macedonia, begging him to come over and help them. Thus, he did not preach in Troas. Now he was in Troas again, and this time the Lord opened a marvelous opportunity for him to spread the gospel. But Paul was under such stress regarding the situation in Corinth that he found it impossible to concentrate on any mission work. Before he could resume his preaching, he felt he had to have word back from Titus concerning the Corinthians (2 Cor. 2:12–13).

Thus Paul left Troas (it was summer of A.D. 56) and headed for Macedonia (Philippi or perhaps even Thessalonica). But things did not go well there either: "This body of ours had no rest, but we were harassed at every turn—conflicts on the outside, fears within" (2 Cor. 7:5). Finally, however, Titus arrived in Macedonia, where he brought word that he had been able to stabilize the situation in Corinth. The Christians there were now longing for Paul and were deeply sorry for what had transpired between them (7:6–7).

Paul was elated! As a result, he wrote his fourth letter to the Corinthian church (2 Cor. 1–8 [or 9]), in which he thanked God for what had transpired and for gifts God had given him to minister the new covenant to them (2:14–6:2). At the same time, Paul knew that the collection had probably been put on hold during the time of tension between him and the Corinthians. Therefore he appended 2 Corinthians 8–9 to his letter, in which he sought to motivate both the Corinthians and the Achaians generally to continue gathering money for the saints in Jerusalem.

From Macedonia to Corinth

Even though the word Paul received from Titus about the Corinthians was good, Paul did not immediately head south to visit that church. Instead, he headed farther west to do more evangelism in areas where no one had yet been—all the way to Illyricum (present-day Bosnia-Herzegovina; see Rom. 15:19–20). In contrast to what had just happened in Troas, Paul was once again able to preach the gospel.

After completing a whirlwind evangelism tour Paul made a final trip through Macedonia to pick up the money he had been collecting for the poor Christians in Judea, and he was thrilled at the results. Even though many of the Macedonians were poor, the Christians in that area had been extremely generous in their giving and felt sorry only that they were unable to give more (2 Cor. 8:1–5).

It was the fall season now, and Paul decided to spend the three winter months in Corinth (Acts 20:2; cf. v. 6). Accompanying him were a number of fellow Christians from both Macedonia and Asia (20:4–5; cf. 2 Cor. 9:4); they would assist him in bringing the money to Jerusalem.

During those three months, Paul began to look to the future again. Since his goal had always been to preach where no one else was preaching (Rom. 15:20–21), he decided that after his quick trip to Jerusalem to deliver the collection, his next mission field would be Spain (Rom. 15:24–25, 28).

A natural stopping point on his way to the western edge of the Roman Empire was the city of Rome itself, which Paul had never visited. Paul therefore decided to introduce himself to the church at Rome and to let them know of his plans to see them (Rom. 1:10–13; 15:23–24, 28). Since he was such a controversial figure in the early church, he felt it was necessary to outline briefly the main points of his theology. To this end he wrote the letter to the Romans during those winter months (early A.D. 57) and sent the letter along with Phoebe, a member of the church at Cenchrea who was probably heading to Rome (Rom. 16:1–2). Paul also took the time to greet every person in the church at Rome he knew—that is, those whom he had met somewhere on his journeys (16:3–15).

Heading to Jerusalem

In spring of A.D. 57, Paul decided to go back to Jerusalem, bringing with him the money he had been collecting in Macedonia and Achaia (Rom. 15:26). He found a ship heading for Syria, but discovered a plot of the Jews (perhaps to steal the money?) just before embarking. Consequently, he quickly changed his travel plans and headed by land back through Macedonia (Acts 20:3). Several of those accompanying Paul went on ahead to Troas while he spent the Passover in Philippi (20:4–6). When he left Philippi by boat for Troas, Luke now also accompanied him. The small company spent seven days in Troas (from a Monday to a Monday; 20:6–7). The night before they left, Paul had communion with the believers there and preached into the wee hours of the morning (20:7–12).

All of Paul's company embarked on a ship at Troas, but Paul once again decided to go overland, this time to Assos, about fifteen miles south. He boarded the ship there. They sailed along the eastern coast of the Aegean Sea, stopping at various places. Paul had decided not to stop in Ephesus, probably because the situation there was still too dangerous and because he would miss his goal of getting to Jerusalem by Pentecost (Acts 20:16). But he did stop at Miletus, about thirty miles south of Ephesus. The group had to spend a couple of days there, so Paul sent word to the elders of Ephesus to meet him in Miletus so he could see them one more time (20:17). Luke records Paul's farewell speech to them (20:18–35). For some reason, Paul felt he would never see them again.

At Miletus, Paul and his friends boarded the ship again and kept on heading south, stopping at various points. At Patara they found a different ship, headed directly to Tyre. After spending seven days in Tyre with the Christians there, they got back on the ship and eventually landed at Caesarea, where they stayed a number of days with Philip (21:1–8).

All along this journey, people kept warning Paul not to go to Jerusalem (21:4, 10–14). But the apostle was determined to present his gift in person to the Christian authorities in the holy city, so he refused to heed these warnings. Arrangements were made for Paul and those with him to stay at the house of Mnason, an elderly Cypriot believer living in Jerusalem (21:15–16). Paul's third missionary journey was now over.

Paul's Imprisonments

Paul and James Meet

As soon as Paul arrived in Jerusalem, he and his friends attended a meeting of their Christian brothers and sisters in that city (Acts 21:17). At that time he presented to the church the generous monetary gift he had been carrying, which had been donated by his Gentile churches (cf. 24:17). The believers in Jerusalem were deeply touched by that symbol of Christian unity, and they received Paul and his companions warmly (21:17).

The next day Paul and his group had an appointment with the leaders of the church in the holy city—James and the elders. Paul "reported in detail what God had done among the Gentiles through his ministry" (21:19). These leaders responded by praising God for the success of Paul's mission.

But the leaders knew that suspicions about Paul remained. Since the time of his last visit to Jerusalem, thousands of Jews in Judea had come to acknowledge Jesus as the Messiah, many of whom remained zealous for the law of God. Rumors among them persisted that Paul was teaching his converts, including Jews, to ignore that law (notably, the practice of circumcision), and that he himself no longer obeyed its requirements (21:20–21). Bringing a gift to Jerusalem, no matter how large, was not going to remove concern on this issue.

Consequently, James suggested a political move on Paul's part. Four Christian men in Jerusalem had recently made a Nazirite vow, which was due to expire (see Num. 6:1–21). If Paul would accompany them to the temple as they completed this vow and would pay their expenses, and if he would himself join in their purification rites (a process that would take seven days, 21:27), everyone could see that Paul had not thrown the law of God to the wind but kept it himself (21:23–24).

Paul readily agreed to this proposal. After all, as he had written to the Corinthians, "To the Jews I became like a Jew, to win the Jews. To those under the law I became like one under the law ... so as to win those under the law" (1 Cor. 9:20). If doing this was going to advance the cause of Christ and his church, Paul was more than happy to go along with the suggestion.

Paul's Arrest

Paul quietly went about the necessary steps for completing his purification rites. On the seventh day he expected to receive the water of atonement and be finished. But then some Jews from Ephesus, in Jerusalem for the celebration of the Feast of Tabernacles, caught a glimpse of Paul in the temple. They had earlier seen him in the city with Trophimus, whom they recognized as a Gentile from their Asian city. Therefore they assumed that somewhere in that inner temple complex Paul had also sacrilegiously brought Trophimus, which was a crime punishable by death.

These Jews from Ephesus began to shout at the top of their lungs, asking for help in punishing Paul, both for his preaching against the law of Moses and for his defilement of the temple. Before long, hundreds of people surrounded the apostle, dragged him from the temple, and immediately shut the gates (Acts 21:27–30). Then they began to pummel Paul, fully intent on killing him right outside the temple gates.

The commander of the Roman troops, probably looking down from one of the towers in the Fortress of Antonia (which overlooked the temple), saw that a riot was breaking out, so he immediately dispatched troops to disperse the crowd (21:31–32). After the soldiers rescued Paul, the commander tried to find out why the people were so angry with him. But to get truth from an angry mob proved impossible, so the commander ordered Paul to be brought inside the fortress.

Just before Paul was about to enter the barracks, he asked the commander, in Greek, for permission to speak to the people. The Roman officer was surprised to hear Paul speaking Greek, and Paul introduced himself. He then turned to address the crowd in Aramaic, telling the story of his life as a Pharisee, his conversion, and his commission to preach to the Gentiles (Acts 21:40–22:21). The reference to God's grace for Gentiles started the shouting again.

The commander then took Paul inside the fortress. In order to get the truth out of him as to what was going on, he decided to flog Paul. But the apostle informed him that he was a Roman citizen; consequently, the Roman officer had Paul imprisoned instead of flogged, still determined to find out what was going on (22:23–29).

Initial Investigation and Imprisonment in Caesarea

The morning after Paul's arrest, the Roman commander (whose name was Claudius Lysias; see Acts 23:26) began his investigation to see what the ruckus the previous day had been about. He ordered the Jewish leaders (the Sanhedrin) to assemble and then brought Paul to them and had him stand before them.

When Paul was asked to speak, he began by insisting that his conscience was clear before God—that is, that he had done nothing wrong. Then, knowing that part of the Jewish Council were Pharisees (who believed in the doctrine of resurrection) and part were Sadducees (who did not), Paul called out, "I stand on trial because of my hope in the resurrection of the dead" (23:6). That did it! Instead of there being an interrogation of Paul, a vehement argument broke out between the two main factions of the Sanhedrin. The Pharisees even stood by Paul and were ready to exonerate him.

The Roman commander terminated the session and had Paul brought back into the Fortress of Antonia. A number of Jews, however, felt that the best way to handle the situation was to assassinate Paul, and they vowed to do so. They developed a scheme: They would ask the commander to bring Paul in for a second meeting with the Sanhedrin; while he was being brought to the meeting (probably accompanied by two soldiers), a group of forty Jews would ambush them and kill Paul (23:12–15).

But Paul had a sister in Jerusalem, and her son somehow heard about the plot. This nephew visited Paul in prison that afternoon to tell him what was happening, and Paul immediately sent him to inform the Roman commander (23:16–21). Thereupon the commander decided to remove Paul from Jerusalem and send him to Caesarea, the Roman capital for Palestine, accompanied by a large regiment of soldiers. He wrote a letter to Governor Felix, explaining as best he could what had been going on (23:25–30). Thus, Paul ended up in prison in Herod's palace at Caesarea.

Paul's First Trial

Five days after Paul's removal from Jerusalem, the high priest and some of the elders traveled to Caesarea, together with a lawyer named Tertullus. Felix opened a court session and allowed Tertullus to bring official charges against Paul. After opening remarks intended to flatter Felix, the lawyer cited three charges: that Paul was a Jewish troublemaker, stirring up trouble wherever he went; that he was a ringleader of an illegal sect—the Nazarenes; and that he had brought a Gentile into a prohibited part of the temple (Acts 24:5–8).

Governor Felix then motioned to Paul, who had no legal representation, to speak. One by one the apostle answered the charges brought against him. He admitted that he was a follower of "the Way," which the Jews called a sect. But this was not an illegal religion, Paul insisted, since it was simply a different way of looking at the Jewish Scriptures. At this time, emperor worship was the established religion, required of everyone; but the Romans allowed certain "old-time" religions (such as Judaism) to be legal. Moreover, Paul was not a troublemaker and had not started a riot in the temple; he was simply going about his religious business privately (24:10–18).

But Paul went on to admit that there were some strong feelings against him from certain Jews from Asia. Tacitly, he was admitting to some troublesome times that he had had with them in Ephesus. But those Asian Jews were not in court to testify against him. More than likely, with the Feast of Tabernacles being over, they had returned home by now. The only possible reason why he was arrested, Paul went on to say, was because he believed in the resurrection from the dead (in particular, the resurrection of Jesus Christ) (24:19–21).

Felix made no decision in the matter but told all concerned that he would take the matter under advisement. He ordered Paul back to prison, but privately with his wife (a Jewess named Drusilla) sent for Paul to listen to what his preaching was all about. For the next two years, he kept Paul incarcerated and met with him periodically. Secretly, Felix hoped that Paul would offer him a bribe for his release (24:24–26). He probably assumed that with the collection Paul had told him about (24:17), the apostle had access to lots of money.

Paul's Second Trial

After two years (early A.D. 59), Felix was replaced as governor by Porcius Festus. Felix had sought to quell hostilities between the Jews and Greeks in Caesarea by killing many Jews and plundering their possessions. When the Jews complained to Rome, the emperor removed Felix from his post as governor.

Festus was a much better administrator than Felix. His first task was to win the support of the Jews, so within three days of being appointed governor, he headed for Jerusalem to meet with the Sanhedrin. One of the issues they raised was their charges against Paul, which had been put on hold. The Jews asked whether Paul could be brought to Jerusalem for trial—and they secretly intended to carry out their assassination plot on the way (Acts 25:2–3). Festus promised to investigate the situation as soon as he arrived back in Caesarea.

A little over a week later, Festus reopened Paul's case and held a court session. The Jews repeated the same unsubstantiated charges they had made two years earlier, and Paul responded the same way he had back then, denying all charges against him (25:6–8). Festus then asked Paul if he was willing to go to Jerusalem to stand trial (25:9). Realizing that he had done nothing wrong and that the only reason why Festus wanted him brought to Jerusalem was to please the Jews, Paul felt he had no other recourse as a Roman citizen than to appeal the case to Caesar (25:10–11). Festus had no choice but to honor Paul's request (25:12).

In the meantime, while arrangements were being made to transport Paul to Rome, King Herod Agrippa II, ruler of the territory north of Palestine, came to Caesarea to pay his respects to the new governor. Since Agrippa was far more familiar with Jewish practices than Festus, and since Festus had no idea how to write the charges against Paul to the Roman emperor, he sought Agrippa's assistance (25:24–27). Agrippa had heard about Paul and eagerly asked if he could meet with him (25:13–22). So the next day, with much pomp and circumstance, Festus arranged for Paul to address a whole group of dignitaries. Paul used the opportunity to present the story of his conversion and to encourage everyone there, especially Agrippa, to become believers (ch. 26).

The Voyage to Rome

It was early fall of A.D. 59 when Festus finally made the necessary arrangements for Paul to be taken to Rome. Paul was put in the care of a centurion named Julius, and they boarded a ship at Caesarea (Acts 27:1–2). They crept along the eastern and then the northern coast of the Mediterranean and eventually landed at Myra, in the Roman province of Lycia. From there they boarded a grain-carrying ship from Alexandria that was headed straight for Rome. Rough winds, however, made it slow going out in the open sea. Thus, they headed for the south shore of Crete, hoping to spend the winter there.

The first port on Crete they stopped at, Fair Havens, did not have a good winter harbor. So when the weather cleared, the captain decided to head for Phoenix, which had a better harbor. But no sooner had they left than the weather turned violent, and within a short time the ship was blown out into the middle of the Mediterranean. For days no one saw either the sun or the stars—only the wind and the rain. The sailors were hoping they would not be swept all the way to the North African coast, where sandbars would wreak havoc on the ship. Over a period of a few days, they threw all their cargo overboard to lighten the vessel.

After a couple of weeks, by listening carefully to the waves breaking over a reef, the sailors sensed they were nearing land. They made a sounding and discovered they were right. But it was night, so they threw out four anchors to hold the ship until daylight. In the morning they did not recognize the island in front of them, but they decided to cut the anchors and attempt to beach the ship. It struck a sandbar far from shore, however, and the furious waves began to break the vessel apart.

The captain and the centurion gave orders to abandon ship. When it was all over, everyone on board the ship made it safely to the shore. The island they had landed on was Malta (28:1), about seventy-five miles south of Sicily. The rescued soldiers and passengers had no choice but to spend the three winter months there. Publius, the chief official of Malta, had a sick father-in-law; Paul visited him and healed him. This allowed him to heal many other sick on the island and, undoubtedly, to preach about Jesus.

Paul in Rome

Early in the spring of A.D. 60, those who had been shipwrecked boarded another Alexandrian ship and headed for Rome. Their first stop was Syracuse, on Sicily; then on to Rhegium, on the toe of Italy. The final stopping place for the ship was the port of Puteoli, where grain ships usually docked. For some reason, the company spent seven days in that town. From there the prisoners who had been on the ship had to travel overland about seventy-five miles on the Via Domitiana to Rome. The Christians at Rome received an advance notice that Paul was on the way, so two groups set out to meet him en route. The apostle took great courage from these gestures.

When Paul finally arrived at Rome, he was allowed to find his own living quarters, where he was placed under armed guard. Few restrictions were imposed on him, so he was allowed to have people come to visit him. Thus, he invited the leaders of the Jews, apparently wanting to have a sort of pretrial conference with them. When they arrived, Paul informed them of his circumstances, including his appeal to the Roman emperor. The Jews admitted they knew about people who believed that Jesus was the Messiah, but said they had received no letters from the high priest or Sanhedrin about Paul or any official charges against him. They did not want to get involved—either in support of Paul or against him.

Paul then invited a larger number of the Jews to come and visit him, so that he could preach to them about Jesus. They stayed an entire day, listening to Paul preach about the kingdom of God and demonstrate from the Scriptures that Jesus was God's chosen Messiah. As Paul had experienced everywhere else, some became believers, while others remained unconvinced. Against the latter group Paul spoke his typical words of judgment, and he told them he was now free to invite Gentiles over to hear his message.

Two Years of Imprisonment in Rome

For the next two years—from spring A.D. 60 to spring 62—Paul stayed in that rented house in Rome. He had a lot of freedom to receive visitors and to interact with them. One set of visitors came from Asia, from the town of Colosse. The church in that town had started while Paul was stationed in Ephesus. Some false teachers were attacking the church, presenting different views of Jesus and suggesting a different way to salvation (cf. Col. 2:1–4, 8). They sought to combine elements of the Jewish religion with some of the new Eastern religions that were coming on the scene. Paul therefore wrote to them the letter of Colossians, stressing the supremacy of Christ as God's firstborn Son, the king of creation, and the only Savior there is.

As Paul wrote this letter, he realized its message had broader implications for the church. Therefore he wrote a more general, circular letter to the Christians in Asia, stressing the importance of Christ as head of the church and God's saving grace as implying the unity of Jews and Gentiles in the church—all are one in Christ. This letter is our letter to the Ephesians.

One person whom Paul led to Christ in Rome was Onesimus, a runaway slave of a man named Philemon, who was probably one of the leaders of the church in Colosse. Paul felt the Christian thing for Onesimus to do was to return to his owner; thus, he wrote a brief letter encouraging Philemon to receive his slave back as a brother in Christ.

The Roman emperor at the time was Nero (A.D. 54–68). The first part of Nero's reign was peaceful and gave promise of a prosperous career, probably because he was under the tutelage of the famous orator Seneca. Nero himself boasted that not a single person had been unjustly executed. After two years of house arrest, Paul finally had his day in court before the emperor. It is possible that he was released without so much as a trial, seeing that the Jewish leaders had more critical issues to deal with, becoming more and more involved with internal problems in Judea and the imminence of revolt against Rome. If Paul had no accusers, his case would be dismissed. In any case, we do know that Paul expected to be released soon (see Philem. 22). Once his house arrest was over, he was free to visit his churches again.

The Last Four Decades
of the First Century

Paul's "Fourth" Missionary Journey

After Paul was released from his imprisonment in Rome, he did not sit back, take it easy, and play it safe. Rather, he set out once again to start new churches and to visit those he had started. His expressed goal after visiting the church in Rome had been to evangelize Spain (see Rom. 15:23–24, 28). It is all but certain that he achieved this goal. Clement of Rome, writing thirty years after Paul's death, stated that the apostle had reached the farthest bounds of the West (1 Clement 5:7). Moreover, since Paul was goal-oriented, we can almost assume he would have fulfilled his desire.

Evidence in the Pastoral Letters—that is, 1 and 2 Timothy and Titus— give firm evidence of some of the places Paul visited after his release from prison in Rome. He wrote these letters after his Roman imprisonment, so that references made in those letters to recent visits to churches were later than those recorded in Acts.

One of the places Paul visited and probably evangelized was the island of Crete. Titus was accompanying him, and when Paul left the island, he left Titus behind to finish the task of organizing the churches started there (Titus 1:5). From there Paul returned to Ephesus (cf. 1 Tim. 1:3), perhaps by way of Miletus (2 Tim. 4:20). Apparently false teachers had infiltrated the church in Ephesus, promoting the same sort of heresy that had afflicted Colosse a couple years earlier. Paul spent some time there dealing with that issue and probably fulfilled his desire to visit Philemon in Colosse (Philem. 22). He then set off for Troas (2 Tim. 4:13) and Macedonia (1 Tim. 1:3), leaving Timothy behind as pastor to continue monitoring the troublesome situation in Ephesus.

From Macedonia, Paul apparently traveled to Nicopolis (a town on the western coast of Greece, on the Adriatic Sea) and spent a winter there (Titus 3:12). Paul had more than likely started a church in Nicopolis when he also evangelized Illyricum (Rom. 15:19). Perhaps, after his visit to Western Greece, Paul paid a visit to the church in Corinth (cf. 2 Tim. 4:20). Eventually, according to tradition, he returned to Rome.

James, the Brother of Jesus

James, "the Lord's brother" (Gal. 1:19; cf. Mark 6:3), played an important role in the history of the New Testament church. During the life and ministry of Jesus, James did not believe in Jesus as the Messiah (John 7:5); but shortly after his resurrection, Jesus made a personal appearance to his brother (1 Cor. 15:7), which must have convinced him otherwise. Between Jesus' ascension and the Day of Pentecost, James was a part of that believing crowd that prayed and waited in the upper room (Acts 1:14).

After Peter's miraculous escape from prison, James took over the leadership of the church in Jerusalem (cf. Acts 12:17; 15:13; 21:18; Gal. 1:19; 2:9, 12). According to various historical sources, he was an extremely pious man, keeping all the traditions of the Jews—so much so that he was respected even by unbelieving Jews. His knees were as hard as a camel's since he was on them in the temple so much, praying and interceding for the forgiveness of God's people (see Eusebius, *Church History* 2.23). His nickname was "James the Just."

But James was also a moderate in the sense that he did not expect everyone to live as he did. He rejoiced in the salvation of the Gentiles through the ministry of Paul (Acts 15:13–19; 21:19–20), and he helped to resolve the question of circumcision and salvation (Acts 15). James was also concerned about personal Christian living. To this end he wrote the letter of James, a treatise on practical Christianity in which he alluded to many of the sayings of his brother, Jesus.

After the death of Festus and before a new governor arrived, the high priest Ananias seized the opportunity to call a meeting of the Sanhedrin and charge James and some others with violating the law—probably because they were Christians. Because of this, James was stoned to death (Josephus, *Antiquities* 20.9.1). Eusebius gives a slightly different version of James's death, stating that he was thrown down from a pinnacle of the temple—from where he had been ordered to denounce Jesus but instead proclaimed him as the Messiah—and was then stoned (*Church History* 2.23). Whatever the details, James died about A.D. 65.

The Writing of the Synoptic Gospels

During the first few decades of the mission of the church, those who preached the gospel (both apostles and evangelists, see Eph. 4:11) passed on a message that they had heard from others and that ultimately had derived from the apostles, who were eyewitnesses of the events concerning Jesus (see Luke 1:1–4; 1 Cor. 15:1–8; 2 Peter 1:12–18). But the apostles were becoming older, and at least some of them had died (see Acts 12:1–2). Thus it became necessary to preserve, in writing, the message of the life, ministry, death, and resurrection of Jesus for future generations. This led to the writing of the Gospels.

According to most scholars, Mark was the first Gospel to be written. Church tradition tells us that, sometime in the early-to-mid-60s, John Mark became a close associate of the apostle Peter. (Peter actually calls him "my son" in 1 Peter 5:13.) Under Peter's supervision, therefore, Mark wrote down the basic message that the apostle had been preaching for so many years (see Eusebius, *Church History* 3.39; 5.8; 6.14). Both Peter and Mark were probably living in Rome by then. Mark's Gospel breathes with the personality of Peter and emphasizes Jesus as the Messiah.

Doctor Luke had been a travel companion of the apostle Paul (see "A Vision of a Man from Macedonia"). Shortly before Paul's death, Luke undertook to write a two-volume history of the events in the first century (the Gospel of Luke and the Acts of the Apostles). He was a careful researcher, using (presumably) Mark as one of his sources but also other oral and written traditions about Jesus (Luke 1:1–4). Luke tended to emphasize stories and sayings of Jesus that showed him to be the Savior of the entire human race—rich and poor, men and women, Jew and Gentile, etc.

Perhaps about the same time, Matthew (one of Jesus' disciples) wrote his Gospel. He, too, probably used Mark as one of his sources, but his emphasis was on how Jesus fulfilled the Jewish Scriptures. His Gospel thus seems to have been directed to the Jewish Christian community in Palestine; it was also intended to convince Jews to put their faith in Jesus as God's promised Messiah. According to Eusebius, Matthew had already written a brief collection, in Aramaic, of the sayings of Jesus (*Church History* 3:39).

Nero and the Deaths of Peter and Paul

Nero was born in December, A.D. 37, and was installed as emperor by the Roman senate when he was only sixteen years old. As mentioned in another unit, the early years of his rule were well received—a period hailed as a Golden Age by Roman poets.

But about five years after assuming his position as emperor, Nero's policies took a dramatic turn for the worse. For example, he had his own mother, who had been one of his chief advisors, put to death. Public support for him diminished, especially in A.D. 64, when a massive fire devastated the city of Rome. Rumors started circulating almost immediately that he had deliberately set the fire, in part to be able to redesign the capital city and expand his palace. Thus, Nero sought a scapegoat, blaming the fire on a minority group that consistently refused to join in pagan celebrations—the Christians. On one documented occasion, Nero crucified a large number of believers, covered them with pitch, and lit them as torches for his night chariot races.

Sometime between A.D. 66 and 68, according to church tradition, Peter and Paul were both arrested in Rome. During his imprisonment Paul apparently had at least two appearances before the emperor (2 Tim. 4:16–18). But with Nero's policy of persecuting Christians, Paul knew the hour of his departure was at hand (4:6–8). According to church tradition (see Eusebius, *Church History* 2.25), Paul was beheaded under Nero.

Peter probably wrote his first letter from Rome (called "Babylon" in 1 Peter 5:13), a letter that frequently mentions the persecution of believers. Mark and Silas were both with him at the time. After his arrest under Nero, according to church tradition (see Eusebius, *Church History* 2.25; 3.1), Peter was crucified, possibly upside down. John, in the appendix to his Gospel, also hints that Peter's death came by crucifixion (John 21:18–19).

In A.D. 68, the Roman senate had had enough of Nero and declared him a public enemy. Shortly thereafter, he committed suicide, and the official persecution of Christians ceased, at least for the next fifteen years.

The Jewish War and the Fall of Jerusalem

During the mid-60s A.D., the Jews were increasingly becoming rebellious against the authority of Rome. Cestius Gallus, a governor of Syria, sought to quell the disturbances, but ended up badly defeated at Beth-Horon. This encouraged the Jews to take further steps toward independence and to prepare for inevitable war with Rome; their chosen leader was Josephus. Upon hearing of these losses in Judea, Emperor Nero commissioned Vespasian (along with the latter's oldest son, Titus) to lead the campaign against the Jews. After winning battles throughout Palestine, the two military commanders launched their siege of Jerusalem (A.D. 68).

But, as noted in the previous section, Rome was in a political uproar during this time. Especially after Nero committed suicide, Vespasian had little choice but to put the siege of Jerusalem on hold. After the ensuing power struggle in Italy in A.D. 69, Vespasian survived to become emperor. He was therefore ready to resume his campaign against the holy city.

Jerusalem at this time, of course, was home to both Jews and Christians (especially Jewish Christians, but also Hellenistic believers). During the late 60s, a Christian prophet in the church delivered an oracle that all the Christians should leave the holy city and flee to the mountains (cf. Mark 13:14–19). During the lull in the siege of Jerusalem, therefore, these believers left for a place called Pella—a town on a plateau about five miles east of the Jordan River (see Eusebius, *Church History* 3.5). A large Christian settlement eventually developed in this city. This means, too, that the Christians did not suffer in the destruction of Jerusalem that took place in A.D. 70, when Titus and his troops finally entered the city and destroyed it by fire, including its temple. Since that time, the Jewish temple has never been rebuilt in Jerusalem.

Jewish Persecution of Christians and the Book of Hebrews

The book of Acts suggests that those who were the most vehement persecutors of Christians during its first few decades were strict and zealous Jews. Another book of the New Testament that reflects on the issue of persecution is the letter to the Hebrews, most likely written shortly before the fall of Jerusalem and the destruction of the temple.

The writer who penned this book probably wrote to Jewish Christians who were living in or around Rome (note the greetings in Heb. 13:24, sent by "those from Italy," i.e., people who had left Italy and were living abroad). When the people addressed by this book had first accepted Jesus as the Messiah, life went on pretty much as normal. They enjoyed legal protection as a Jewish sect, and they were able to engage in daily work and earn a decent living.

But things changed. Perhaps the Jewish authorities were finally able to convince the Roman officials that Christians were no longer a Jewish sect (see the next section). Perhaps the persecution under Emperor Nero was beginning. In any case, being a Christian was becoming dangerous, for some believers were being publicly insulted and persecuted, while others were put into prison and their homes ransacked (see Heb. 10:32–34). Many, therefore, were inclined to stop attending worship gatherings (10:25) and perhaps even give up their Christian faith altogether and return to the "safety" of Judaism.

Thus, the main intent of the author of Hebrews was to show the spiritual danger that lurked for anyone reverting to Judaism. Jesus Christ is greater than all those important persons and institutions that were at the heart of Judaism—such as Abraham, Levi, Moses, Joshua, the high priest, the Sinaitic covenant, and the sacrifices. He is the only Savior there is, and to return to Judaism inevitably involved the loss of one's salvation (2:1–4; 6:1–6; 10:26–31; 12:25–29). It is far better to imitate the heroes of faith, even if that meant suffering persecution and death (ch. 11). The readers must never forget that what was awaiting them was not an earthly city but "a heavenly one" (11:16), "whose architect and builder is God" (11:10).

Separation from the Synagogue

After the temple was destroyed, Judaism had little choice but to organize itself around the synagogue, as it presumably had done after the destruction of the first temple centuries earlier. The Pharisees, the only Jewish group that survived the disaster of A.D. 70, undertook this reorganization. Acts indicates clearly that Christians had, until now, frequently continued to worship in synagogues, since they believed in Israel's God. But now the Jewish leadership devised a method of driving Christians out of the synagogue.

This method involved the daily recitation of the Eighteen Benedictions, a series of blessings to the Lord recited by Jews personally every day and in the synagogue weekly. Under the leadership of Rabbi Gamaliel II in about A.D. 80, the following words were added to the twelfth benediction: "For apostates let there be no hope. The dominion of arrogance do thou speedily root out in one day. And let Nazarenes [Christians] and the sectarians perish in a moment. Let them be blotted out of the book of the living. And let them not be written with the righteous. Blessed art thou, O Lord, who humblest the arrogant." The assumption was that no Christian either listening to or reading these benedictions would feel comfortable. Thus, confessing Jesus as Messiah meant leaving the Jewish synagogue community.

The results of this can hardly be underestimated. In "The Gallio Episode" (see above), we noted how the Roman government had differentiated legal and illegal religions. Since Christianity had been considered a sect of Judaism, it received protection as a legal religion. But with the Jews clearly making a distinction between themselves and Christians, it now became possible for Roman officials to persecute the latter. This did not begin immediately after the revision of the Benedictions, but by the beginning of the second century, in some areas of the Roman Empire, official persecution of Christians was well under way.

This is brought to light by a letter of Pliny to Emperor Trajan (10.96) and Trajan's response (10.97), written about A.D. 110. The emperor specifically instructed Pliny not to hunt out Christians for legal prosecution. However, if any individuals (perhaps Jews?) were to bring charges against those who were Christians, Pliny was then to investigate; if the charges proved true, the Christians were to be severely punished if they did not recant their beliefs.

John, the Beloved Disciple

According to church tradition, the last disciple of Jesus to die was the apostle John (cf. John 21:20–23). He spent his early years in the city of Jerusalem, where he was considered one of the "pillars" of the church (see Gal. 2:9). Precisely when he left the holy city we do not know, but he had certainly left before the lull in the siege of Jerusalem toward the end of the seventh decade.

Also according to tradition, John ended up in Asia Minor, where he served as pastor of the church in Ephesus. This was probably not before the death of Paul in about A.D. 68, for Paul had installed Timothy as pastor there (see 1 Tim. 1:3). It is likely that John served in the 70s and 80s, not only as the pastor of Ephesus, but also in a supervisory role for the seven churches in Asia Minor (see Rev. 1–3).

By this time the first three Gospels (Matthew, Mark, and Luke) were circulating in the churches. But there were so many more things that Jesus had done that had not been recorded (cf. John 20:30–31; 21:25). Thus, John took it upon himself to record some of his memories of Jesus.

He did so for a specific purpose. False teachers were emerging in the church who denied the full humanity of God's Son. One of these, whose name (according to Irenaeus) was Cerinthus, suggested that the Christ came upon the man Jesus at his baptism and left him shortly before his death. In response, John emphasized how Jesus, the Son of God, was fully human and fully divine (see especially John 1:1–18).

Another goal John had in writing his Gospel was to strengthen believers who were being persecuted by the Jews and who were being tempted to give up the faith (cf. 8:42–47; 12:37–47; Rev. 2:9–10; 3:8–10).

John also wrote three letters that are now a part of the New Testament. There he specifically mentions that "many antichrists have come" (1 John 2:18). Such false prophets started within the church but eventually left it (2:19). John, therefore, wanted his readers to be able to "test the spirits to see whether they are from God" (4:1; cf. vv. 1–6). This was especially important because many churches did not have regular pastors but were visited occasionally by traveling prophets, and believers had to have a way of identifying who were deceivers and who were authentic preachers of God's Word (see 2 John 7–11; 3 John 5–10).

Developments in Church Organization

During the first century of the Christian era, the church experienced phenomenal growth. From its small beginnings in Jerusalem on Pentecost, it branched out into virtually all areas of the Roman Empire. Such a dramatic increase in size, numerically and geographically, brought with it problems of organization. The apostles, of course, served as the initial organizers and leaders of the church, but as time went on, more were needed.

Acts 6 records the problem with the distribution of food to the widows, which led to the choosing of the Seven to handle this task. Paul attempted to supervise his growing numbers of churches and solve their problems by writing letters, sending emissaries, and appointing leaders whom he trusted. But the apostles were dying, and new problems, such as the threat of heresy, were beginning to afflict the churches. The latter part of the first century, therefore, saw an increasing need for rules and church organization.

When the apostle Paul wrote the Pastoral Letters in the mid-60s, he lay down specific guidelines as to who could become elders and deacons (see 1 Tim. 3; Titus 1:5–9). The letters also gave instructions on the role of the leading elder or pastor (Timothy and Titus), on care of the widows, and on payment for those who held church office.

During the last decade of the first century, trouble erupted in Corinth (a church that had had a long history of difficulties). A rebellion broke out against certain long-time elders of the church, who were subsequently removed from office and replaced by younger presbyters. On hearing this, Clement, leader of the church at Rome, took it upon himself to write a letter to the Corinthians (1 Clement) and to send a delegation to restore peace and order. This is the first evidence of a new phenomenon—one church (in the capital city, Rome) seeking to intervene and lord itself over another church (in Corinth).

Also about this time, The Didache was written, a document that spelled out certain liturgical rules on baptism and the Lord's Supper, gave instructions on how to differentiate between true and false visiting teachers, and cited regulations on worship and choosing elders and deacons. This document claimed to have the backing of the twelve apostles.

The Domitian Persecution of Christians and the Book of Revelation

Between the reigns of Nero (A.D. 54–68) and Domitian (81–96), Christians were relatively free from persecution, at least on an imperial level. But things gradually changed when Domitian, a son of Vespasian, became emperor. Usually, a Roman emperor was declared a god upon his death, but Domitian wanted to be honored and worshiped as "Lord and God" while he was still living.

As always, of course, Jews were exempted from the requirement to worship any other god besides their own God, Yahweh. But with the Jews having devised a way to expel Christians from the synagogue, the latter no longer enjoyed the legal protection afforded the Jews. Consequently, there were now legal grounds for commanding Christians to acknowledge the emperor as lord and god or else be subject to severe persecution. Christians refused to do so, of course, for to them Jesus was God and Lord. Both pagan and Christian sources attest to Domitian's hostility to Christianity (see Eusebius, *Church History* 3.17–18), sending believers into exile and confiscating their property.

This new reality is evident in the book of Revelation. The writer himself, the apostle John, had been exiled from Ephesus to the island of Patmos because of his refusal to denounce Jesus (Rev. 1:9). Believers in the church at Smyrna (2:8–11) had been put out of the synagogue and were now suffering persecution and great poverty. In Pergamum, Antipas was killed for refusing to renounce his faith (2:12–13). By contrast, churches such as Laodicea were apparently capitulating under persecution, for they retained their wealth—but were charged by John with being lukewarm in their faith (3:14–17).

Some of the other references in Revelation are perhaps veiled allusions to this Domitian persecution, at least as a type of the final persecution of God's people in the Tribulation. For example, the writer points out that many saints have been "slain because of the word of God and the testimony they had maintained" (Rev. 6:9). Moreover, the saints are commanded to worship the beast, who has made war against them (13:1–8); in refusing to do so, they are called to patient endurance and faithfulness (13:9–10). When all is said and done, however, Christ will win out and be victorious over all his enemies (Rev. 19). Amen. Come, Lord Jesus (22:20).

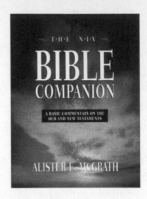